Do Dogs Dream?

"Coren is your go-to guy when you're seeking information about canines. Here, he brings both his expertise and a certain cheeky flair to 75 questions about the social and emotional lives of dogs."

—*Library Journal*

"In this breezy and conversational book, Coren concisely answers your queries about all things dog. Great fun!"—Patricia McConnell, PhD, CAAB, author of *The Other End of the Leash*

"Two paws up for a great read and fascinating information about man's best friend." —Nicholas H. Dodman, BVMS, DACVB, author of *If Only They Could Speak*

"Dog lovers always wonder what their dogs think. Do they dream? Get jealous? Irritated? Coren answers all of our questions in a delightfully clear and readable way. After reading this book, you will dazzle fellow dog walkers and play-group members. Finally, you can know what your dog is thinking." —Jon Katz, author of *A Good Dog*

"Authoritative, lively, and a joy to read, *Do Dogs Dream?* is essential reading for every dog owner. This informative, myth-busting book will answer all your questions—and more—about our canine companions." —Sam Gosling, PhD, author of *Snoop: What Your Stuff Says About You*

ALSO BY STANLEY COREN

STANLEY COREN

Do Dogs Dream?

Nearly Everything Your Dog Wants You to Know

W. W. NORTON & COMPANY

NEW YORK LONDON

For information about permission to reproduce selections from this book,
write to Permissions, W. W. Norton & Company, Inc.,
500 Fifth Avenue, New York, NY 10110

For information about special discounts for bulk purchases,
please contact W. W. Norton Special Sales at
specialsales@wwnorton.com or 800-233-4830

Manufacturing by RR Donnelley, Harrisonburg
Book design by Ellen Cipriano
Production manager: Julia Druskin

Library of Congress Cataloging-in-Publication Data
Coren, Stanley.
Do dogs dream? : nearly everything your dog wants you to know / Stanley
Coren.— 1st ed.
p. cm.
Includes bibliographical references and index.
ISBN 978-0-393-07348-5 (hardcover)
1. Dogs. 2. Dogs—Psychology. I. Title.
SF426. C677 2012
636.7'089689—dc23
2012011404

ISBN 978-0-393-33812-6 pbk.

W. W. Norton & Company, Inc.
500 Fifth Avenue, New York, N.Y. 10110
www.wwnorton.com

W. W. Norton & Company Ltd.
Castle House, 75/76 Wells Street, London W1T 3QT

1 2 3 4 5 6 7 8 9 0

To Bam Bam, Loki,

Bishop, Corey, Sadie, Charley,

Maggie, Wiley, Jane, Barley, Slater,

Doodles, Elvis, and Cosmo—

friends who recently went away

and are missed.

Contents

PART 2

DO DOGS REALLY THINK AND HAVE FEELINGS?

PART 3

HOW DO DOGS COMMUNICATE?

PART 4

HOW DO DOGS LEARN?

PART 5

IS THERE SOMETHING SPECIAL
ABOUT PUPPIES AND OLD DOGS?

PART 6

WHAT ELSE DOES MY DOG WANT ME TO KNOW?

Preface

THERE ARE SO many questions that most of us would like to ask our dogs about their behaviors, their origins, and their nature. Unfortunately, dogs tend to keep their secrets and never answer our queries directly.

As a psychologist and behaviorist, I have been studying and doing research on the behavior of dogs for nearly half a century. I've published a dozen books on dogs and several hundred articles, in addition to having the television show *Good Dog!*, which was broadcast nationally in Canada for more than a decade. Since people know that I've done such extensive work with dogs, they're always asking me questions about particular quirks in their dog's behaviors. They want explanations for some of the strange things that dogs tend to do on a regular basis. They also want insights into dogs' nature, personality, and emotional makeup, in addition to information about what sort of intellectual activity might be going on inside their dogs' furry skulls.

The same questions seem to crop up again and again, as though they make up the core of information that we would like to know about our favorite pets, and perhaps what our dogs would like us to know about them if we could have an intimate conversation with them. This book attempts to answer most of those questions, and in the process it will expose you to some of the more interesting findings that researchers have discovered about dogs but that, for some reason, have not yet become common knowledge.

PART 1

How Do Dogs
Perceive the World?

Do Dogs See Colors?

T HE SIMPLE ANSWER —namely, that dogs are color-blind— has been misinterpreted by people as meaning that dogs see no color, but only shades of gray. This conception is wrong. Dogs do see colors, but the colors they see are neither as rich nor as varied as those seen by humans.

The eyes of both people and dogs contain special light-catching cells, called "cones," that respond to color. Dogs have fewer cones than humans have, suggesting that their color vision is not as rich or intense as ours. However, the trick to seeing color is not just having cones, but having several different types of cones, each tuned to different wavelengths of light. Human beings have three different kinds of cones, and their combined activity allows us to see the full range of colors that characterizes human vision.

The most common types of human color blindness come about because one of the three kinds of cones is missing. An individual with only two cone types can still see some colors, but many fewer than someone with normal color vision sees. This is the situation with dogs, who also have only two kinds of cones.

Jay Neitz at the University of California, Santa Barbara, tested the color vision of dogs. For many test trials, dogs were shown three light panels in a row—two panels of the same color, and a third that was a different color. The dogs' task was to press the panel that was different in color. Correct responses were rewarded with a treat that the computer delivered to the cup below that panel.

Neitz confirmed that dogs actually do see color, but many fewer colors than normal humans do. Instead of seeing the rainbow as violet, blue, blue green, green, yellow, orange, and red, dogs would see it as dark blue, light blue, gray, light yellow, darker yellow (sort of brown), and very dark gray. In other words, dogs see the colors of the world as basically yellow, blue, and gray. They see the colors green, yellow, and orange as yellowish, and they see violet and blue as blue. Blue green appears gray.

One amusing or odd fact is that the most popular colors for dog toys today are red or safety orange (the bright orange red on traffic cones or safety vests). However, red is difficult for dogs to see. It may appear as a very dark brownish gray or perhaps even a black.

This means that that bright-red dog toy that is so visible to you may often be difficult for your dog to see. When your own pet version of Lassie runs right past the toy you just tossed, the problem may not be that the dog is stubborn or stupid, but that you chose a toy with a color that is hard for a dog to discriminate from the green grass of your lawn.

How Good Is a Dog's Vision?

VISUAL ACUITY IS a measure of how small a visible detail can be and still be identified by a person. The most common way of testing vision is to use an eye chart (the kind you see in an optometrist's office that has the big "E" in the top row). This chart is known as a *Snellen Eye Chart*, because it was designed by Hermann Snellen in the late 1800s. It uses symbols that are formally known as "optotypes." Optotypes have the appearance of block letters and are intended to be seen and read as letters. They are not, however, letters from any ordinary typographer's font collection. They have a particular, simple geometry in which the sizes of lines, gaps, and white spaces are carefully determined so that if you can't see them clearly enough, the letters become confusing and difficult to read. The letters (and the white spaces and gaps that define them) get progressively smaller as you move down the chart. The line with the smallest letters that you can read is a measure of your visual acuity or, more specifically, your eye's detail-resolving ability.

The number assigned to your acuity is based on how you compare to a person known to have normal visual acuity. If you are tested at a distance of 20 feet and can read the same line of letters that a person with normal vision can read at 20 feet, then the Snellen measure of your vision is 20/20 (or 6/6 if you're measuring the distance in meters). If your vision is not that good, then you will need the letters printed larger to read them at that distance. For example, if the letters that you can just barely read correctly at 20 feet are large enough that a person with normal vision can read them at 40 feet, your vision is 20/40 (or 6/12).

Obviously we can't get a dog to read rows of letters for us, so we use another technique for determining a dog's visual acuity. In this test we want the dog to demonstrate to us that he can see the details that define a pattern. The pattern we use for dogs is a simple grid made up of equal-sized black and white vertical stripes. We put this pattern up next to a uniform gray pattern. Dogs who have vision good enough to see the striped pattern and who correctly pick out that pattern get a treat. Dogs who pick the gray pattern get nothing. Next we run the test with stripes that become narrower and narrower. This test is equivalent to making the letters on the eye chart smaller and smaller. Eventually the stripes will be so thin that the dog's visual acuity will not allow him to see that the stripes are there. At this point the stripes blur and smear in the eye, and the

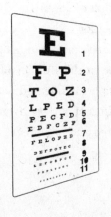

card with the stripes will look the same as the card with the uniform field of gray. When the size of the stripes just arrives at this point, we have reached the limits of the dog's visual acuity. The size of the stripes that the dog can see can be converted to the same Snellen acuity measure that we get from an eye chart used to test people.

The highest acuity documented to date with this kind of acuity measure comes from a Poodle tested in Hamburg, Germany. Even this dog's acuity, however, was quite poor; he was able to make out only those patterns having stripes that were nearly six times wider than the minimum that humans can make out. Converting this result to the more usual measures, the dog seems to have had a visual acuity of only 20/75. This means that a pattern that a dog can barely recognize at 20 feet (6 meters) is actually large enough for a person with normal vision to identify at a distance of 75 feet (23 meters). For a sense of how poor this vision is, consider the fact that if your visual acuity was worse than 20/40, you would fail the standard vision test given when applying for a driver's license in the United States and would be required to wear glasses. A dog's vision is considerably worse than 20/40.

Don't let these numbers fool you, however. Although the dog's visual acuity is considerably less than that of a normal human, a lot of information is still getting from the dog's eyes to its brain; it's just that the focus is "soft" and the dog can't make out many details. The effect is something like viewing the world through a fine-mesh gauze or a piece of cellophane that has been smeared with a light coat of petroleum jelly. The overall outlines of objects are visible, but a lot of the internal details will be blurred and might even be lost.

Why Do Dogs' Eyes Glow in the Dark?

Y OU MAY HAVE noticed that at night, when a dog's eyes are caught by car headlights or in a flashlight beam, they seem to glow with an eerie yellow or green, making the dog look like some sort of hellhound. The reason has to do with the fact that the wild canines that dogs evolved from are "crepuscular," meaning that they are usually active at dusk and dawn and therefore need eyes that work well in dim light. Their eyes are thus somewhat different from those of people.

Understanding eyes is a bit easier if you think of a camera. Both your eye and a camera require a hole to let light in (the shutter aperture in the camera, and the pupil in the eye), a lens to gather and focus the light, and some kind of sensitive surface to register the image (the film or photodetecting layer in the camera, or the retina in the eye). Both eyes and cameras need features that allow them to adjust to various light conditions, and both are continually making compromises between working well at low levels of light and being able to see small details. At every stage in the construction of the dog's eye, the choice seems to have been made to sacrifice some ability to see small or fine aspects of the environment in order to be able to function better at low light levels.

When it comes to letting light into the eye, your dog's pupils are much larger than those of most humans. In some dogs you can't really see much of anything except the wide pupil filling the eye, with just a hint of colored iris around the edge. Because of their larger lenses, dogs' eyes also have more light-gathering power than human eyes have.

To gather a lot of light, a lens has to be big, which is why astronomical telescopes, such as the one at Mount Palomar in California, can have lenses as large as 200 inches (500 centimeters) across. Effectively two parts of the eye serve as lenses in humans and dogs. The first is the "cornea," which is the transparent portion of the eye that bulges out at the front. The cornea is responsible for the actual light gathering. The second part, the "crystalline lens," is behind the pupil and is responsible for changing the focus of the light. Animals that are active in dim light usually have large corneas. Notice how large your dog's corneas are in comparison to those of people. This larger size permits more light to be gathered and sent into the eye for processing.

Light passing through the pupil and the crystalline lens eventually forms an image on the retina. Here much of the light is caught and registered by special neural cells called "photoreceptors." As in human beings, the dog's retina contains two types of photoreceptors: "rods," which are long and slim; and "cones," which are short, fat and tapered. Rods are specialized

to work under dim light conditions. Not surprisingly, dogs have a much higher proportion of rods in their eyes than humans do, but they also have an additional mechanism to meet the needs of night hunting that is not found in humans.

Now we get to the reason why a dog's eyes glow like eerie yellow or green headlights when a light beam hits them at night. This color comes from the reflecting "tapetum," which is behind the retina and acts as a sort of a mirror. The shiny surface of the tapetum bounces any light that has not been caught by the photosensitive cells back up to the retina, thus giving the photoreceptors a second chance at catching the dim light entering the eye.

More than simply reflecting the light, the tapetum actually amplifies it through a photoelectric phenomenon called "fluorescence." Fluorescence not only adds to the light's brightness but also slightly changes the color of the light that is reflected back. The color shift moves the wavelength of the light closer to the wavelength that the rods are most sensitive to and can best detect, which is a yellowish green.

Although the light bouncing off of the tapetum increases the sensitivity of the eye, there is a cost. The light that hits that reflective surface in the back of the eye comes from various directions and, like a pool ball hitting the bumper edge of the table, it does not return along exactly the same path it followed as it entered, but bounces off at an angle. Because the incoming direction of the light and the reflected direction are different, images on the retina are smeared and appear to be a bit blurred. Thus, the dog's eye has clearly chosen to sacrifice its ability to see fine details so that it can function better in dim and dark conditions.

Do Dogs Understand
What They See on Television?

MANY PEOPLE REPORT that their dogs completely ignore what is visible on television, while others report that their dogs are often captivated by events on the TV screen. Whether or not a dog pays attention to a program on television depends on a number of factors, but mainly on the dog's visual abilities. If we reduce the events that we see on the TV screen to their simplest form, the motion that we see really becomes a changing pattern of light across the retina in our eye. At the level of single cells on the retina, a moving target appears to be a flicker. As the image of the target passes over a visual receptor in the eye and then moves on, it causes a momentary increase or decrease in brightness. For this reason, behavioral researchers often use an individual's ability to see a flickering target as a measure of not only the speed at which the visual system can record events, but also of the efficiency of motion perception.

To measure flicker sensitivity, an individual looks at a lighted panel. If the rate of flickering is very fast, there is "flicker fusion" and the panel looks the same as if it were a constant, unchanging illumination. A fluorescent light, for instance, seems to be glowing continually with a uniform light, but it is actually flashing at a rate of 120 times (cycles of light and dark) per second. In the laboratory, the ability to resolve flicker is measured by slowing the flicker rate until the person begins to see the light flutter. When humans are tested on this task, the average person can't see any flickering much above a speed of 55 cycles per second, or about half the rate that fluorescent lamps normally flash. (Technically, the number of cycles per second is referred to as hertz, abbreviated Hz.) It is possible to test dogs using this same task. On average, Beagles are able to see flicker rates up to 75 Hz—about 50 percent faster than the flicker rate that humans can resolve.

The fact that dogs have better flicker perception than humans have is consistent with the data suggesting that they perceive motion better than people do. It also answers a commonly asked question: Why do the majority of dogs seem uninterested in the images on television—even when those images are of dogs? The answer is that the image on a raster television screen is updated and redrawn 60 times per second. Since this rate is above a human's

flicker resolution ability of 55 Hz, the image appears continuous and successive images blend smoothly together. Given that dogs can resolve flickers at 75 Hz, to dogs a TV screen probably appears to be rapidly flickering, making the images appear less real and thus causing many dogs not to direct much attention to them. Even so, some dogs seem to ignore the apparent flickering of the television and respond to dogs and other moving images on the TV screen if they're interesting enough. However, changes in technology are beginning to change the number of dogs that watch TV. High-resolution digital screens are refreshed at a much higher rate, so even for dogs there is less flicker, and we are getting increasing reports of pet dogs who are very interested when a nature show contains images of animals moving.

Still, people are sometimes surprised to find that although their dog responds when there is a dog on the screen, or perhaps some other animal running swiftly, it does not respond to cartoon images of dogs. This distinction really is a testimony to how well dogs see and accurately interpret moving images. On seeing a cartoon canine, a dog recognizes that the figure is moving, but the movements of an animated figure are not a precise rendering of the pattern of movements of a live animal. Therefore, the dog sees something moving but recognizes that it is not a dog or any other real animal of interest.

How Do You Test a Dog's Hearing?

T RYING TO DETERMINE what a dog is hearing was difficult until some recent scientific innovations came onto the scene. If you want to know what a person is hearing, the testing procedure is straightforward. You simply present sounds at different frequencies (high, low, and medium pitches) and at varying intensities and ask whether the individual hears them. To determine the hearing ability of dogs (or other animals) using a similar behavioral method, the researcher first has to train the animal to respond to the location of the sound. Specifically, the dog is put in a test apparatus that has a speaker and a panel or a lever on both the left and right sides of the dog. The experimenter presents a sound to either speaker randomly. If the dog hears the sound, its task is to decide which side the sound came from. If, after making that decision, the dog presses the lever under the correct speaker, a treat is delivered to a cup below that speaker. If the decision is wrong, the dog gets no treat for that test trial. The training and testing using this method are tedious, extending over many weeks of training and hundreds of test trials.

More recently, a hearing test known as the "brainstem auditory evoked response" (BAER) has been used to measure hearing in dogs. This procedure detects electrical activity in the inner ear (the cochlea) and in the neural pathways that send the sound infor-mation to the brain. Researchers attach tiny electrodes to the dog's scalp and fit him with earphones or a little sound-emitting device inserted in the ear. It sounds ugly and painful but it's not, and it's easily done with a relaxed dog, although some fidgety or sensitive dogs do have to be mildly sedated.

During testing, short bursts of sound are delivered to the ear, and the brain's response is recorded by a computer. The computer deter-mines whether the brain responded to the sound. If the brain did not respond, researchers can assume that the dog did not hear it. The advantage of this test is that dogs don't have to be trained over a long period. In fact, the dog doesn't even have to know what is going on, since scientists are simply looking at the brain's response to sounds.

Actually, simply observing your dog's behavior can provide clues about whether his hearing is failing—which is a commonplace occur-rence in older dogs. Quite often, the first sign of hearing impairment in dogs is an inability to locate sounds accurately. This deficit may show up as confusion when you call your dog and he can't see you. The dog may look around uncertainly, coming only when he finally catches sight of you. Another sign is that when a loud sound is heard, the dog may swing his head first to the wrong side, away from the direction that the sound occurred. Sometimes this loss of sound localization is the only noticeable symptom indicating that your dog has lost the hearing in one ear, although the other ear is still functioning.

If you're worried about your dog's hearing, there are some simple tests you can do at home. First, stand behind him, out of sight, and squeeze a squeaky toy, whistle, clap your hands, or bang a metal spoon against a pot. A dog with normal hearing will prick its ears or turn its head or body toward the source of the sound. Be very careful not to stand directly over the dog, since dogs are sensitive to air currents and may feel your movements or the vibrations in the floor immediately behind them. Also make sure that the dog hasn't seen you before you make the sound. Sometimes it is best to conduct these tests when your dog is sleeping, to reduce the likelihood that the dog is responding to the sight of your movements.

It is not sensible to try home tests of a dog's hearing in a very young puppy. Dogs are not born with all of their exquisite hearing abilities fully matured. Measurements taken in puppies aged eleven to thirty-six days show that their hearing, although functioning at birth, improves with age over the first month or two. An interesting additional fact is that the puppies' ability to hear higher-frequency sounds improves more rapidly that their ability to hear low- or middle-pitched sounds. So if you're concerned about a puppy's hearing, wait until the dog is about five weeks old before conducting hearing tests.

The ability to hear sharp, high-frequency sounds is what the dog's ear was designed for; it is his most resilient hearing ability and is often the last aspect to go when a dog's hearing declines. A sharp clap of the hands, or a quick blast on a loud whistle, will often produce an ear flick and a turn of the head that lets you know your dog heard you, even if he can no longer make any sense of human voice sounds.

Compared to a Human,
How Good Is a Dog's Hearing?

IF YOU BROWSE the Internet, you will often see it written that dogs' hearing is four times more acute than ours, which is not strictly true. This statement comes from an informal experiment conducted by P. W. B. Joslin, whose research involved monitoring the activities of timber wolves in Algonquin Park. Joslin discovered that captive wolves responded to his own attempts at howling from a distance of 4 miles away, whereas, even on a quiet night, his attempts at howling could not be heard by his human colleagues from more than about a mile away. The fact that a canine can hear sounds coming from four times farther away than a person can is probably what led to this interpretation. The truth of the matter, however, is that for some sounds a dog's hearing is really hundreds of times better than ours, while for other sounds dogs and humans have sound sensitivities that are about the same.

As we noted in the previous section, determining what a dog is hearing was difficult until the BAER hearing test was developed. The big surprise from extensive electrophysiological testing of canine hearing using this new method was that in the middle range of sound frequencies, which make up human speech sounds, dogs and humans have virtually identical hearing sensitivity. For lower-frequency sounds, human beings are actually more sensitive. The intensity of sounds is measured in decibels (abbreviated dB), where zero decibels is the average intensity of a sound that can just barely be heard by a young human being. Any intensity that is less than zero is written with a minus sign in front of it and usually represents a sound that is too faint for average humans to hear. For sounds with a frequency of 2,000 hertz (Hz) and all of the frequencies below this, down to a low pitch of about 65 Hz, dogs and humans have about the same hearing sensitivity. From about 3,000 to around 12,000 Hz, dogs can hear sounds that average between –5 and –15 dB, meaning that they are considerably more sensitive to these higher-frequency sounds than people are. Above 12,000 Hz, human hearing ability is so bad relative to that of dogs that it doesn't make sense to compare them numerically.

To get a better picture of what's going on, you should understand that, roughly speaking, a young human being can hear sounds up to 20,000 Hz. If you wanted to have a piano that could produce this highest hearable sound, you would have to add about twenty-

eight keys to the right-hand side of the keyboard (about three and a third octaves). Don't bother trying to create such a piano, however, because most people will not be able to hear the highest notes anyway. As we age, the pounding of sound waves against the mechanisms in our ears causes mechanical damage, and we lose the ability to hear higher-pitched sounds first. Exposure to loud sounds (too many rock concerts or too many hours listening to tapes or CDs played at high volume) quickly reduces hearing ability, especially in this high range, so that few adults hear above 16,000 Hz.

Dogs can hear considerably higher pitched sounds than people can. The highest ranges are between about 47,000 to 65,000 Hz, depending on the characteristics of the dog. To return to our modified piano, we would have to add forty-eight extra notes to the right-hand side of the keyboard to reach the top note that a dog can hear, and the last twenty notes would be completely undetectable by even the most sensitive human ear.

The fact that dogs have greater sensitivity to sounds than humans do, especially in the higher frequencies, helps explain why some common sounds—like those made by vacuum cleaners, motorized lawn mowers, and many power tools—can cause great distress in dogs. Many of these types of equipment have quickly rotating shafts on the motors that power fans, blades, or bits. This kind of arrangement can produce intense high-frequency "shrieks," which for dogs can be painfully loud, while our less sensitive human ears are not bothered, because these shrieks are at much higher frequencies than our ears can register.

Dogs can hear sounds in the very high frequency range because of the evolutionary history of their wild ancestors. Wolves, jackals, and foxes often prey on small animals like mice, voles, and rats. These prey animals make high-pitched squeaks, and their scrabbling around in the leaves and grass produces high-frequency rustling and scraping sounds. Although some wild canine species, such as the wolf, can and will hunt larger prey like deer, wild sheep, or antelope, field studies show that the summer diet of many wolves is composed mainly of small rodents like rats and mice, supplemented with an occasional rabbit. The ability to hear the high-frequency sounds that these little creatures make is therefore a matter of survival, and only those canines that developed high-frequency hearing abilities were more likely to survive and prosper. Cats, whose entire sustenance may depend on small rodents, can hear sounds that are 5,000–10,000 Hz higher than the highest sounds that dogs hear.

How Sensitive Is a Dog's Sense of Smell?

A DOG'S NOSE DOMINATES not only his face, but also his brain. While the human brain is most strongly oriented toward analyzing data from the eyes and information gathered through light, the dog's mind is designed with an emphasis on gathering information from scents. The part of the dog's brain that is devoted to analyzing smells is proportionally forty times greater than that of humans.

Dogs work more actively than humans to gather scents. They don't let smells casually drift into the nose, but use certain abilities that humans don't have. To start with, dogs can move or wiggle their nostrils independently, which helps them determine the direction a scent is coming from. Dogs also have a special sniffing ability that is quite different from their normal breathing. When your dog pushes its nose in the direction of a scent, he actively interrupts the normal breathing process so that the material he has sniffed passes over a bony shelflike structure in the nasal cavity that is designed to trap the odor-containing air and protect it from being washed out when the dog exhales. This mechanism allows scent molecules to remain in the nose and accumulate to the point that there are enough of them for the dog to recognize.

The bony plates in the dog's nose are covered with a thick, spongy membrane, which contains most of the scent-detecting cells and the nerves that will take the information up to the brain. For humans, the area containing these odor analyzers is about one square inch, the size of a postage stamp. If we could unfold the corresponding area in the dog's nose, it might be as large as 60 square inches, or just about the size of a piece of typing paper. In part because of this difference in the number of scent-detecting cells, it has been estimated that dogs can identify smells somewhere between a thousand and ten thousand times better than humans can.

Although dogs are more sensitive than humans to virtually all scents, their noses are specially attuned to animal-related odors. You might have expected this to be the case, since dogs are hunters and should be tuned to the kinds of odors their prey would tend to leave behind. We see one example when we compare the human sensitivity for butyric acid, which is a component of sweat, to that of a dog. Humans are pretty good at detecting this odor at the reasonably low concentration of about one five-millionth of a gram evaporated into a cube of air that is one meter square. Although that sounds pretty impressive, consider the fact that if we dissolved this same amount of butyric acid in 250,000 gallons of water, a dog would still be capable of detecting it. If we took 1 gram of butyric acid and let it evaporate in the volume of a ten-story building, when you opened the door your human nose would be only just barely able to smell it. If we evaporated that same gram of butyric acid in the air and dispersed it over a 135-square-mile area and up to a height of 300 feet in the air, a dog would still be able to smell it. This is approximately the same size as the area covered by the entire city of Philadelphia! Since that city contains about one and a half million people, all of whom sweat (especially on typically hot, muggy summer days), it is interesting to speculate what that metropolis must smell like to a dog.

Do Some Dog Breeds Have
Better Noses Than Others?

ALTHOUGH ALL DOGS have fine scent recognition abilities, their talents can be improved through selective breeding. The Beagle, Basset Hound, and Bloodhound are good examples showing that sensitivity to odors is, at least partly, genetically determined. These dogs have been bred as specialists, with not only a special ability to detect and discriminate scents, but also a passion to follow, track, and explore odors.

The bony ridge inside the dog's nose that contains the smell-detecting cells varies in size, depending on the overall size of the dog's nose. Dogs with longer and wider noses have more of this surface available; dogs with smaller noses or flat faces and short noses, like Pugs and Pekingese, have a smaller surface area in this portion of the nose and therefore simply don't have the room for as many scent-detecting cells. For example, Dachshunds have about 125 million smell receptor cells, while Fox Terriers have 147 million and the German Shepherd Dog has about 225 million.

Some dogs, in particular the dogs that we call "scent hounds," have noses that are designed to be very wide and deep in order to pack the largest number of odor-analyzing cells into the available space—even if the dog itself is not very large. Thus, the very scent-oriented Beagle, which normally weighs in at only about 30 pounds and stands only 13 inches at the shoulder, has the same 225 million scent receptors as the German Shepherd Dog, which is twice the size of the Beagle, at 75 pounds and a height of 24 inches. The grand champion of scenting is the Bloodhound. These big-nosed dogs check in at about 300 million scent receptors in their noses.

How do the numbers of scent-detecting cells in dogs compare with those in humans? Human beings are not very smell oriented, in part because we have noses that contain a paltry 5 million smell-analyzing cells. In other words, the average human being has a nose that contains only 2 percent of the number of odor-analyzing cells that can be found in the nose of the little Beagle.

The dog's scent-detecting ability has one additional quirk: for reasons that are not completely clear, male dogs seem to have better scent discrimination than female dogs. Some behavioral scientists have suggested that this is not because the male dog's nose is more sensitive than the female's, but rather because he is simply more interested in and focused on smells, such as the scent of a female dog who is in heat or may be sexually receptive.

Can Dogs Detect Cancer?

T HERE HAVE BEEN many anecdotal reports about dogs detecting cancer, such as the case of Arlene Goldberg of Chicago. She owes her life directly to her Cocker Spaniel, Duffy, who developed an annoying habit of jumping up on her and sniffing and nipping at a mole on the back of her shoulder near the base of her neck. Duffy was so persistent that Arlene mentioned it to her doctor, who removed the mole and had a biopsy done. A few days later Arlene was back in the hospital to have the surrounding skin removed because the mole turned out to be a virulent form of melanoma that could have killed her if it had metastasized. The original set of medical reports analyzing case studies like Arlene's first appeared in the respected medical journal the *Lancet* in 1989. Since then, a number of controlled experimental studies have confirmed that dogs can detect cancer as well as, or even better than, traditional medical screening techniques.

One of the first studies was conducted by the Florida dermatologist Armand Cognetta, who decided to investigate possible medical uses of dogs in cancer detection. In 1996, Cognetta borrowed a seven-year-old Schnauzer named George (a recently retired bomb-sniffing canine), with the goal of determining whether the dog could consistently sniff out melanoma, in both tissue samples and people. Normally, a handheld microscope is used to diagnose potential skin cancer, and a biopsy usually follows. Because observation with a microscope is only about 80 percent effective in early diagnosis (meaning that one in five diagnoses will be wrong), further tests are generally conducted to confirm the cancer. Using tissue samples of melanomas from research institutes and a hospital, Cognetta trained George to find a tube containing a melanoma sample. George eventually became quite proficient, so that when the melanoma sample was placed in one of ten holes in a large rectangular box, with the other holes containing normal tissues, the dog could find the melanoma 99 percent of the time. Cognetta then allowed George to "examine" actual patients, which is considerably more difficult. Eventually, George discovered melanoma in four (possibly five, depending on how you look at the results) of seven patients. These results were interesting but far from conclusive, so a set of larger and more controlled studies seemed to be called for.

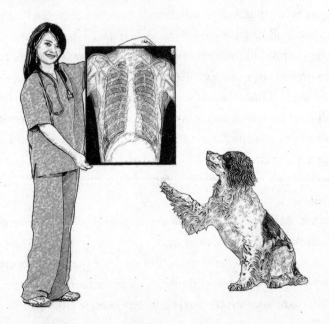

Carolyn Willis of Amersham Hospital in England, along with her associates, conducted a meticulously controlled, double-blind study showing that dogs can be trained to recognize and indicate bladder cancer. They used sets of six urine samples belonging to patients who were either healthy or suffered from another disease, plus a sample from patients with bladder cancer. Neither the researchers doing the testing nor the dogs being tested had any way of knowing in advance which sample was cancerous until after the dogs made their choices.

In one instance the dogs kept identifying a sample that medical staff had asserted was cancer-free. Willis said, "The trainers just couldn't train the dogs past this particular sample at all. They were really getting quite desperate that this wasn't going to work. Because the dogs consistently went for that one sample, we went back and conferred with a specialist."

Andy Cook, one of the trainers, describes what happened next. "The hospital had seen our dogs' work and had got confidence in our dogs, sent it off for further tests. They were completely blown away when it came back that this patient not only had cancer on his kidney but there was also bladder cancer."

Some dogs seem to spontaneously recognize cancer, but recent work shows how quickly and effectively dogs can be trained to find this malignancy. Michael McCulloch of the Pine Street Foundation in San Anselmo, California, together with his colleagues, needed only three weeks of training to teach five pet dogs to detect lung or breast cancer by sniffing the breath of participants. The trial itself involved eighty-six cancer patients (fifty-five with lung cancer, and thirty-one with breast cancer) and a group of eighty-three healthy patients. In the study, the dogs sniffed breath samples captured in special tubes. Dogs were trained to sit or lie down directly in front of a test station with the cancerous sample. The results were spectacular, showing that dogs can detect breast and lung cancers with an average of better than 90 percent accuracy.

In a new study, Hideto Sonodo of Kyushu University in Japan collected breath and stool samples from patients with colorectal cancer, also known as bowel cancer. The researchers placed one cancerous sample and four noncancerous samples in storage containers, and in a series of "sniff" tests they commanded a Labrador Retriever to search for the container that held the cancerous sample. The dog sniffed out the cancerous sample in thirty-three out of thirty-six breath tests, and in thirty-seven out of thirty-eight stool tests. That's almost as accurate as a colonoscopy test for colorectal cancer. Furthermore, in some cases the samples had come from patients with early stages of bowel cancer, which are notoriously difficult to detect.

A trained dog has the potential of screening more than twelve thousand people for cancer in its lifetime, making the investment of time to produce cancer-detecting dogs good economics, as well as good medicine. Perhaps sometime in the future, that "lab test" you get for possible cancer may well come in the form of some educated sniffing by a Labrador Retriever.

How Good Is a Dog's Sense of Taste?

I F YOU BELIEVE the dog food commercials on television, dogs are very sensitive to taste. Taste is a very old sense in evolutionary terms. It evolved from direct interactions of the first living things with the giant bowl of chemical soup in which they were immersed. The substances that were suspended or dissolved in water were important to the survival of these primitive living things. Some substances provided food, some gave warning, and some could cause damage or even kill. As animals evolved, the taste system became more specialized and sophisticated. Sensations of pleasure and disgust provided by taste serve a survival function. A reasonable rule of thumb, at least for natural substances, is that bad tastes indicate something harmful, indigestible, or poisonous, while good tastes signal useful, digestible substances.

Because it is important for survival, taste is, not surprisingly, one of the earliest senses to begin functioning in dogs. Young puppies seem to have only their senses of touch, taste, and smell working at birth, although the taste sense still requires a few weeks to completely mature and sharpen.

As with humans, the dog's sense of taste depends on special receptors called "taste buds." These are found on the top surface of the tongue in small bumps called "papillae." There are some taste buds in other places as well, such as the soft part of the roof of the mouth (the "palate") and the back part of the mouth where the throat begins (the "epiglottis" and the "pharynx"). An animal's taste sensitivity depends on the number and type of taste buds it has, in much the same way that sensitivity for smell depends on the number of olfactory receptors. Humans win the sensitivity contest for taste, with about 9,000 taste buds, compared with only 1,700 for dogs; but dogs have considerably more taste buds than cats, which average only about 470.

Specific taste buds appear to be tuned to specific chemical groups and produce recognizable tastes. Traditionally, when talking about human tastes, we've identified four basic taste sensations, corresponding to the tastes that we call sweet, salty, sour, and bitter. Although early research did show that the taste receptors of dogs respond to the same kinds of chemicals that trigger human taste sensations, there is one clear difference, having to do with the taste

of salt. Humans, and many other mammals, have a strong taste response to salt. We seek it out, and we like it on our food. Pretzels, potato chips, and popcorn, for example, are snack foods that are usually liberally dosed with salt. Salt is needed to balance our diet, and not much of it is to be found in vegetables and grains. Dogs are different, since they are primarily carnivores and in the wild most of their food is meat. Because of the high sodium content in meat, the wild ancestors of dogs already had a sufficient amount of salt in their diet and did not develop our highly tuned salt receptors and the strong craving for salt.

Dogs are not exclusively carnivorous, but are sometimes classified as omnivores, meaning that they eat not only meat, but plant material as well. Nonetheless, in the wild more than 80 percent of a canine's diet will be meat. For this reason, in addition to having sensors for sweet, salty, sour, and bitter, dogs have some specific taste receptors that are tuned for meats, fats, and meat-related chemicals. Dogs tend to seek out and clearly prefer the taste of things that contain meat or flavors extracted from meat.

The sweet taste buds in dogs respond to a chemical called furaneol. This chemical is found in many fruits and also tomatoes. Cats are virtually "taste-blind" for this substance. It appears that dogs do like this flavor, and the taste for it probably evolved because in a natural environment dogs frequently supplement their diet of small animals with whatever fruits happen to be available.

The taste buds for the basic flavors are not distributed equally across the tongue. Sweet is best tasted at the front and side portions of the tongue. The sour and salty taste buds are also on the sides, but farther back, with the salt-responding area being rather small. The rear portion of the tongue is most sensitive to bitter tastes. Sensitivity to meaty tastes is scattered over the top of the tongue, but found mainly in the front two-thirds. However, all areas of the tongue can respond to all of the taste stimuli if the stimuli are strong enough;

it's just that the areas specifically mentioned here are noticeably more sensitive to the particular tastes identified.

Because of dogs' dislike of bitter tastes, various sprays and gels have been designed to keep dogs from chewing on furniture or other objects. These compounds often contain such bitter substances as alum or various substances derived from hot peppers. Coating items with bitter-tasting material will eventually keep most dogs from chewing on them, but the key word is "eventually." Part of the problem is that the taste buds that sense bitter are located on the rearmost third of the tongue. This means that a quick lick or a fast gulp will not register the bitter taste. Only prolonged chewing will let the bitter work its way back to where it can be tasted.

Dogs also have taste buds that are tuned for water—a characteristic that they share with cats and other carnivores but that is not found in humans. This taste sense is found at the tip of the dog's tongue, the part of the tongue that the dog curls to lap water. This area responds to water at all times, but when the dog has eaten salty or sugary foods, the sensitivity to the taste of water increases. This ability to taste water is believed to have evolved as a way for the body to keep internal fluids in balance after the animal has eaten things that either will result in more urine being passed, or will require more water for adequate processing. This taste sense is useful, since dogs are carnivores and, as we already mentioned, meat has a high salt content. It certainly appears that when these special water taste buds are active, dogs seem to get an extra pleasure out of drinking water, and they will drink copious amounts of it.

Why Do Dogs Have Whiskers?

PROTRUDING FROM THE sides of a dog's muzzle is a set of stiff hairs that are popularly called whiskers or, more technically, "vibrissae." These are not at all like the nonfunctional whiskers that men sometimes grow on their faces. Cats have similar hairs that people often refer to as "feelers," which may be a better name, since vibrissae really are sophisticated devices that help the dog feel its way through the world. Vibrissae are quite different from most other hairs on the dog's body, in that they are considerably more rigid and embedded more deeply in the skin. At the base of each vibrissa is a high concentration of touch-sensitive neurons.

Vibrissae are found in a variety of animals other than dogs, including cats, rats, bears, and seals, suggesting that they must serve a useful function. One way to determine how important something is to an animal is to see how much of the brain it uses. Of those areas of the brain that register touch information in the dog, nearly 40 percent is dedicated to the face, with a disproportionately large amount of that area dedicated to the regions of the upper jaw, where the vibrissae are located. We can actually map each individual vibrissa to a specific location in the dog's brain, suggesting that great importance is assigned to information from these structures.

The vibrissae serve as an early warning device that something is near the face; thus, they prevent collisions with walls and objects, and they keep approaching objects from damaging the dog's face and eyes. You can demonstrate this for yourself by tapping gently on the vibrissae of a dog. With each tap, the eye on the same side of the face will blink protectively, and the dog will tend to turn its head away from the side tapped.

The vibrissae also seem to be involved in the location of objects, and perhaps in the recognition of the objects themselves. Most animals use vibrissae in much the same way that a blind person uses a cane. First, the little muscles that control the vibrissae direct them somewhat forward when the dog is approaching an object. Next they actively "whisk" (vibrate slightly) while the dog swings his head to drag these hairs across surfaces. Whisking gives information about the shape and roughness of surfaces near the dog's head. Since the dog's eyes can't focus very well on close objects, and his muzzle blocks his line of sight when the dog is looking at things near his mouth, the information from the forward- and downward-pointed vibrissae appears to help the dog locate, identify, and pick up small objects with his mouth.

Many dog fanciers are unaware of the importance of vibrissae to

dogs, and most groomers seem to consider vibrissae a purely cosmetic feature, as if they were the same as human facial hair. Dogs of many different breeds routinely have their vibrissae cut off in preparation for the show ring. It is argued that this grooming technique gives the dog's head a "cleaner" look. Unfortunately, amputating vibrissae is both uncomfortable and stressful for dogs, and it reduces their ability to perceive their close surroundings fully.

Specifically, dogs whose vibrissae have been removed seem more uncertain in dim light. Under these conditions dogs move more slowly, because they are not getting the information they depend on to tell them where things are that they might bump into. With intact vibrissae, the dog actually does not have to make physical contact with a surface to know it is there. These special hairs are so sensitive that they also register slight changes in air currents. As a dog approaches an object like a wall, some of the air that he stirs up by moving bounces back from surfaces, bending the vibrissae slightly, which is enough to inform the dog that something is nearby well before he touches that thing.

Do Dogs Sense Pain the Way Humans Do?

IT WAS BARELY ten years ago that I found myself sitting in a scientific conference listening to a veterinarian who claimed, "Dogs do not feel pain to the same degree that people do, and therefore the idea of assessing and managing pain in dogs is not very important."

The myth that dogs don't feel pain like humans do, or at least that they don't feel as much pain as we do, is partly the result of a legacy from the wild origins of our dogs. Canines have inherited an instinct to hide any pain that is caused by injury or infirmity. In the wild, an animal that is injured or infirm is vulnerable to attack, and there is a survival advantage to acting like nothing's wrong even when something most definitely is. Thus, our pet dogs still appear to act in a stoic manner. They suppress many of the more obvious signals of pain and injury to protect themselves and their social standing in their pack. They hide their pain so that they appear more in control of the situation, but unfortunately this instinctive behavior makes it difficult for we humans to recognize when our dogs are hurting.

Many veterinarians accept the idea that dogs have a low sensitivity to pain—except for certain "wimpy breeds." The behavior of veterinarians is consistent with this belief. Several surveys have shown that even after surgical operations, such as abdominal procedures and spaying or neutering, approximately half of all vets send the dog home without any medication to control pain.

Some vets even argue that a little pain is good for an animal that needs to rest, since it keeps the animal quiet and prevents excessive activity. However, consider the comparable human situation in which a woman has had a hysterectomy (basically the same procedure as spaying a dog). Imagine how she would respond if her physician refused to prescribe any medication for her and said, "The pain will be good for you because it will keep you still and quiet while you're healing."

The research literature is quite clear in showing that pain, especially if it is experienced over a long duration of time, can actually be hazardous to a dog's health. The reason is that pain is a stressor, and in response to stress the body begins to release a set of stress-related hormones. These hormones affect virtually every system in the body, altering the rate of metabolism, causing neurological responses, and inducing the heart, thymus glands, adrenal glands, and immune system to go into a high state of activity. If this situation continues long enough, these organs may actually become dysfunctional. In addition, the tension that the state of pain-related stress induces can decrease the animal's appetite, cause muscle fatigue and tissue breakdown, and also rob the dog of needed, healing sleep. In the end, the dog is exhausted as well as distressed, and this state reduces the body's ability to heal.

Researchers have been

studying the effects of controlling or managing pain from injuries, illness, and surgical procedures in dogs. When scientists looked at the recovery of dogs that have undergone surgery, they found that treating the dogs with drugs to control their postsurgical pain produced major benefits that include improved respiratory functions, decreased stress responses surrounding surgery, decreased length of hospitalization, faster recovery to normal mobility, improved rates of healing and even a decreased likelihood of infection after surgery. Almost all studies show that people and animals return to normal eating and drinking habits sooner when given relief from pain.

The researchers sum up their results by suggesting that prevention, early recognition, and aggressive management of pain and anxiety should be essential to the veterinary care of dogs. They warn us that it is important to be sensitive to the subtle signs of pain in our pets because the treatment of that pain itself can be healing by reducing the stress that can prolong recovery.

With that in mind, it is important for you to know the signs and symptoms of pain in your dog. You may be a better judge of whether your dog is hurting than your veterinarian is, simply because there is nothing better than being familiar with an individual dog in order to recognize how its behavior has changed and how it shows pain.

Generally speaking, dogs that are hurting appear less alert and more quiet than normal. They may hide to avoid being with other animals or people. They may have stiff body movements and show an unwillingness to move. Like people in the same situation, a dog in severe pain might lie still or assume an abnormal posture to reduce its discomfort. In cases of less severe pain, dogs may appear restless and more alert, and they may start pacing around.

Dogs in pain will show signs of stress, which include panting and shallow breathing. They may shiver, and the pupils of their eyes may be larger than usual. In addition, you can be pretty sure something's wrong if your dog stops eating normally. Contrary to what you might expect, dogs do not bark more when they're in pain; however, they are more likely to whimper or howl, especially if left alone.

A dog in pain may engage in unexpected growling if someone approaches, and it may appear more aggressive. Part of this altered behavior might simply be an attempt to guard or protect parts of the body that hurt.

While any of these changes in your dog's behavior may mean that your pet is in pain, some of these symptoms also might mean that your dog is anxious, nervous, or in poor health. As such, they are early warning signs that should prompt you to take your pet in for a proper medical examination.

Remember, the longer your dog is in pain, the longer his recovery may take, because of the side effects of pain-related stress. The good news, though, is that there are now many more good and effective ways to manage and control pain in your dog.

Do Dogs Recognize
Themselves in a Mirror?

M
ANY PEOPLE ARE puzzled by the fact that dogs seem to ignore images of themselves reflected in a mirror. Young puppies encountering mirrors for the first time may treat the image as if it were another dog. They may bark at it, or give a little bow and an invitation to play as if they were encountering a real dog and engaging in a social interaction. After a short while, however, they lose interest. Later they often seem to treat their reflections as if they are of no consequence at all.

When we humans look into a mirror, we immediately recognize that the image we're gazing at is our own. It seems so natural that we tend not to think about it as something special, but psychologists treat this as a major mental feat because it requires self-awareness, which is one of the most sophisticated aspects of consciousness. In effect we must be able to mentally step outside of ourselves and consider ourselves as entities separate from the rest of the world.

We are not born with the ability to recognize ourselves in mirrors. Young infants may be fascinated by their reflection, but they view such an encounter as a social interaction with what appears to be another baby. Sometime between the ages of eighteen and twenty-four months, babies begin to understand that they're looking at themselves in a mirror. To demonstrate this phenomenon, Jeanne Brooks-Gunn and Michael Lewis surreptitiously placed rouge spots on babies' faces. If the baby thinks that the image in the mirror is another child, the red spots evoke little interest. However, once the baby understands that he's looking at his own image, he will begin to selectively touch and explore those spots while looking at the mirror, because now he understands that the image is a representation of himself.

Gordon Gallup, a psychologist from the State University of New York at Albany, did a similar experiment on chimpanzees. First he introduced a mirror into the home cage of a chimpanzee. Initially the chimp reacted as if it were seeing another individual, but over time it learned that this was its own reflection. Next Gallup anesthetized the chimpanzee and painted a red mark on its eyebrow and another over its ear. When the anesthesia wore off, the chimp failed

to show any interest in the marks until it caught sight of itself in the mirror. On seeing its image with the red marks, the chimp began to act like children who know that they're looking at themselves in the mirror: touching its own eyebrow and ear while carefully watching its image in the mirror. Gallup believes that this behavior means the chimp is self-aware. It understands that it is an individual and that the reflection it sees is one of itself.

Orangutans, gorillas, and dolphins respond with the same evidence of self-awareness when presented with mirror images of themselves. Dogs and other species, however, either treat the image as another animal or come to ignore it completely. The conclusion that researchers drew from the fact that dogs fail the face mark and mirror test is that dogs lack self-awareness, and thus consciousness. Another conclusion that could be drawn, of course, is that dogs recognize the reflection as their own but are simply not as vain and concerned with their appearance as higher primates are.

University of Colorado biologist Marc Bekoff offered an alternative way of interpreting these apparently negative results. He recognized that dogs are considerably less affected by visual events than are humans and most apes. Perhaps the difficulty resides with the sensory modality used to test self-awareness in dogs. The most important sense for dogs is not sight, as in primates, but rather smell. Dogs certainly seem to recognize the scent of familiar dogs and people, and if they have a sense of self, then perhaps rather than asking them to recognize their own reflection, we should ask them to recognize their own scent. Instead of a "red dot test" for self-awareness, Bekoff used a "yellow snow test." His subject was his own dog, Jethro, a cross between Rottweiler and German Shepherd Dog. He described the clever, but rather inelegant experimental process this way:

> Over five winters I walked behind Jethro and scooped up his yellow snow and moved it to different, clean, locations some

distance down the trail. I also gathered yellow snow from other dogs and moved it. There is a real advantage to doing this experiment on snow because it holds the urine and is easily portable. Since it took five winters to get all of the data, you know that this was a labour of love.

All of this snow moving occurred while Jethro was elsewhere along the path, and the dog did not see Bekoff transporting it. The testing was quite simple: Bekoff watched Jethro move down the trail, timed his arrival, measured how long the dog sniffed at the urine patch, and watched what else he did. As most dog owners could probably have predicted, the dog stopped at each yellow snow patch, sniffed at it, and then usually urinated on top of the yellow snow from other dogs. However, Jethro seemed to recognize his own scent, since when he encountered his own urine-stained snow, he sniffed at it for a much shorter time than he did the patches of urine from other dogs, and then he left it alone.

Bekoff's observations led him to conclude that dogs do have some of the same aspects of self-awareness that humans have. According to him, they have a sense of "body-ness," which is the feeling of possessing one's own body and owning the parts of that body—"my paw," "my face," and so on. In addition, dogs have a sense of "mine-ness," which is the sense of what belongs to oneself and what belongs to others—"my territory," "my sleeping place," "my bone," and so on. What this data cannot establish is whether dogs have a sense of "me-ness," which, for lack of a more concise way of describing it, is what Tarzan was talking about when he said, "Me Tarzan, you Jane." An experimental test for that quality of self-awareness in dogs does not yet seem to have been worked out, but using a mirror clearly won't work, since reflected images have no scent and therefore are not real or important enough in the mind of a dog to warrant much attention.

PART 2

Do Dogs Really Think
and Have Feelings?

Do Dogs Have the Same Emotions That People Have?

M OST DOG OWNERS can look at their pet and easily tell whether he or she is happy, angry, afraid, or depressed. The emotional state of our dogs often seems quite obvious. For that reason, it is difficult for many people to understand that the existence of emotions in dogs was (and in some places still is) a point of scientific controversy.

Several forces led to a disbelief in animal emotions. Perhaps the most important was that in the sixteenth and seventeenth centuries, scientists were learning that living things are composed of systems that follow chemical and mechanical rules. This realization led the French philosopher and scientist René Descartes to suggest that animals like dogs are simply some kind of machine, filled with the biological equivalent of gears and pulleys. This machine doesn't think, but it can be programmed to do certain things. Nicolas de Malebranche, who extended Descartes's ideas, summed up the concept when he claimed that animals "eat without pleasure, cry without pain, act without knowing it: they desire nothing, fear nothing, know nothing."

You might argue against the conclusions of these theorists by pointing out that if you challenge a dog, it obviously becomes angry

and snarls or snaps, or it becomes fearful and runs away. The scientists of Descartes and Malebranche's time, and their successors,
would say that the dog is simply acting, not feeling. Dogs are programmed to snap at things that threaten them or, if the threat is too
great, they are programmed to run away. You might point out that
if you kicked a dog, it would yelp in pain and fear. These researchers might then respond that if you kicked a toaster, it would make
a sound. Is this a yelp of pain indicating that the toaster is afraid?
Their argument would be that, like toasters, dogs simply act but do
not feel.

Science has progressed, and we have now come to understand
that dogs have all of the same brain structures that produce emotions in humans. Dogs have the same hormones and undergo the
same chemical changes that humans do during emotional states.
Dogs even have the hormone oxytocin, which, in humans, is
involved with love and affection for others. Given that dogs and
people have the same neurology and chemistry, it seems reasonable
to suggest that dogs also have emotions similar to ours. However, it
is important not to go overboard and immediately assume that the
emotional ranges of dogs and humans are the same.

The key to understanding the emotions of dogs comes from
research on people. Not all humans have the full range of emotions.
In fact, infants have a very limited emotional range. Over time,
though, the infant's emotions begin to differentiate and develop,
and by the time they're adults, humans have a range of emotional
experiences that is quite broad. As we'll see later in this book,
research suggests that the mind of a dog is roughly equivalent to
that of a human who is two to two and a half years old. A child of
that age clearly has emotions, but not all possible emotions.

The accompanying illustration charts the development of human
emotions in the first five years of life. At birth, a human infant has
only one emotion, which we might call excitement. Excitement indi-

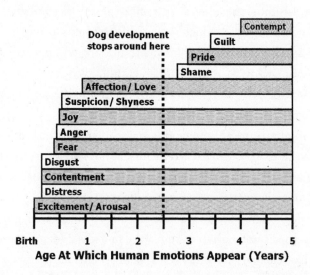

Age At Which Human Emotions Appear (Years)

cates the infant's level of arousal, ranging from very calm up to a state of frenzy. Within the first weeks of life, the excitement state comes to take on a positive or a negative flavor, so we can now detect the general emotions of contentment and distress. In the next couple of months disgust, fear, and anger become detectable in the infant. Joy often does not appear until the infant is nearly six months old, and it is followed by the emergence of shyness or suspicion. True affection, the sort that can be labeled as "love," does not fully emerge until nine or ten months of age. Complex emotions—those with elements that must be learned—don't appear until later. Shame and pride take nearly three years to appear, while guilt appears about six months after that. A child must be nearly four years old before it feels contempt.

This developmental sequence is the golden key to understanding the emotions of dogs. Dogs go through their developmental stages much more quickly than humans do, attaining all of the emotional range that they will ever achieve by the time they're four to six months old (depending on the rate of maturing in their breed).

However, we know that the assortment of emotions available to the dog will not exceed that which is available to a human who is two to two and a half years old. This means that a dog will have all of the basic emotions: joy, fear, anger, disgust, and even love. However, a dog will not have the more complex social emotions, like guilt, pride, and shame.

You might argue that your dog has shown evidence of feeling guilt. In the usual scenario, you come home and your dog starts slinking around and showing discomfort, and you then find his smelly brown deposit on your kitchen floor. It is natural to conclude that the dog's actions show a sense of guilt about its transgression. However, this is not guilt, but simply the more basic emotion of fear. The dog has learned that when you appear and his droppings are visible on the floor, bad things happen to him. What you see is the dog's fear of punishment; he will never feel guilt.

So, feel free to dress your dog in that silly costume for a party. He will not feel shame, regardless of how ridiculous he looks. He will also not feel pride at winning the prize for wearing that bizarre getup. However, your dog can feel love for you, and contentment when you're around.

Does Genetics Determine a
Dog's Personality?

PSYCHOLOGISTS USE THE word "personality" to mean those characteristics people display that allow us to predict how they will behave, react, and feel in various situations. Some scientists, however, are uncomfortable using the word "personality" when talking about nonhuman animals. They use the word "temperament" instead, and although the average person sees little difference between the two, using a different label allows the scientist to suggest that there are significant qualitative differences between the behaviors of people and animals.

What, however, is personality, and what leads to personality differences among dog breeds—indeed, even among individuals within breeds? Biology teaches us that two main ingredients contribute to making all of us what we are: genetics ("nature") and the environment ("nurture"). In dogs, a large proportion of personality is due to inherited genes.

How dog personality is genetically controlled was the focus of exploration by Jasper Rine of the University of California, Berkeley, among others, as part of the Dog Genome Project that is mapping the genetic code of dogs. Rine began his research with a Border Collie named Gregor (after Gregor Mendel, the nineteenth-century monk credited with some of the earliest insights into the science of genetics) and a Newfoundland named Pepper (because she's black), who were bred to each other.

Rine chose Border Collies and Newfoundlands not only because they are physically different but because they have very different personalities. Newfoundlands are easygoing and affectionate dogs, protective of people, loyal, and not easily startled by noises or distracted by things going on around them. They are not overly active and would rather walk than run. Border Collies are much the opposite. Although friendly enough, they are far more devoted to their work than to the people around them. They are intense and focused, yet easily upset by sudden, attention-grabbing events going on around them. When you enter a room, a Newfoundland may nudge you, asking for attention and affection; a Border Collie is more likely to acknowledge your arrival with a glance and then return to his task of trying to herd the cat.

Gregor and Pepper's puppies (called the "F1" generation) were given personality tests. The five indicators that the project looked at were (1) demand for affection, (2) excitement barking, (3) startle response, (4) sociability with other dogs, and (5) likelihood of staring or "showing eye" (a dominance behavior, especially strong in Border Collies, that is used to exert influence over other animals and people).

In general, the puppies fell somewhere in the middle between their parents—more affectionate and easygoing than their Border Collie father, but more intense and excitable than their Newfoundland mother. However, when members of the F1 generation were mated to each other (to create the "F2" generation), the personality traits began to sort themselves out in unpredictable ways. One of the F2 puppies seemed to be very demanding of affection and not easily startled (both of which are Newfoundland personality characteristics), but it was not very sociable around other dogs, seldom barked, and used lots of threat stares (Border Collie personality traits). Another pup was very affectionate with people and sociable with other dogs (Newfoundland characteristics) but made lots of dominant eye contact and startled easily (Border Collie traits). Yet, as with its parents, this dog's barking was an average of the characteristics of its grandparents—more than a Newfoundland but less than a Border Collie.

The twenty-three members of the F2 generation exhibited just about every possible combination of the personality characteristics of their grandparents. These characteristics had averaged out in their F1 parents. But as the genes recombined, some breed-specific characteristics emerged again in recognizable form and strength, but in combinations never observed in the purebred grandparents.

This research not only demonstrates genetic control of dog personality characteristics, but also has implications for breeders of "designer dogs" such as so-called Cockapoos or Labradoodles. If, for instance, the aim is to create a dog with a blend of the characteristics of Cocker Spaniels and Poodles, this blend will reliably occur only in a first-generation breeding of purebred parents. Subsequent generations can be quite unpredictable in both temperament and physical characteristics.

Why Are Some Dogs So Anxious and Fearful?

ALLIE WAS A Pomeranian and as brave and self-reliant as one could expect for a dog of that size—at least until you brought out a toaster, inserted a piece of bread, and clicked it on. That simple act would cause the dog to flatten its ears, whimper, and run and hide. A psychologist would say that Allie had developed an extreme fear or phobia associated with the toaster. While this is an odd thing to be fearful of, many dogs develop phobias associated with a variety of circumstances. Most typically, we find dogs that are afraid of loud noises, such as thunderstorms and fireworks, but also they can become fearful of children, men, riding in cars, going down stairs and such, or esoteric things, such as butterflies or flickering shadows.

The signs indicating that a dog is experiencing fear or anxiety include body language such as flattened ears, tail lowered between the hind legs, cowering, slinking, yawning, hair raised on the back of the neck, trembling, drooling, or panting. The dog may also cling to the owner, whine and whimper, or even dribble puddles of urine. In extreme cases the dog may show distressed behaviors, ranging from pacing and destructive chewing to growling or snapping at individuals who are the source of its fear, or even at its owner or other family members.

Although some dogs are born with a genetic predisposition toward fearfulness, most fears that we encounter in dogs are due to experiences that they've had during their lifetime or experiences that they've failed to have at certain times in their development. Probably the most important single factor in whether your dog develops into a confident or a fearful animal is its early socialization.

Socialization is simply the process by which a young dog has experience with a variety of people, places, and situations while it is still young. There is a fairly narrow window of opportunity to socialize the dog. After eight weeks of age, puppies start to become shy and wary of unfamiliar people, and this tendency must be dealt with before the puppy reaches fourteen weeks of age. A second window opens between five and eight months of age, when dogs become fearful of strangers and will often single out certain groups, such as children or men, as the target of their fear. This condition worsens quickly, and it may turn into aggression. If such fears are not nipped in the bud, you may end up with a dog whose life is burdened with enough stress and anxiety to make him useless as a working, competition, or protection dog, and perhaps even as a satisfying companion dog.

Shy and fearful dogs can be rehabilitated to some degree, but it takes a lot of work, and they will never be as reliable as a well-socialized dog. Fortunately, the process of socialization is really quite easy and enjoyable. The idea is to safely and pleasantly expose the puppy to all sorts of different people, strangers, men with beards, children, people wearing glasses, smokers, people who are old, the infirm, those who use walkers or canes, people carrying bags, and so forth. The pup should also be exposed to a variety of different places, different rooms, paved streets, parking lots, public buildings, gas stations, and any other places that the dog is likely to encounter. Lots of treats, petting, happy talk, and interactions with friendly people will make the dog glad to engage in such exercises. Although the pace of these new experiences can ratchet down after the puppy reaches the age of eighteen weeks, they should not stop until you've made it all the way through the second window of time—that is, until the pup is about nine months to a year old.

While using socialization to prevent fears from developing in the first place is the ideal situation, there is always the possibility that a later traumatic event will cause a fear or phobia to arise. That appears to be the situation in the case of Allie and her fear of toasters. Apparently her owner was preparing breakfast one day and had just clicked on the toaster, when a contractor who was helping to remodel their home, dumped a large quantity of construction materials in the driveway beside the kitchen, causing a loud and frightening clatter. From that point on, the click of the toaster and the smell of browning bread would send Allie into a panic.

What do you do if your dog has already developed a fear or phobia? The most natural response is to treat dogs much the way we would treat young children who were acting fearful—namely, to comfort them. With dogs, however, this is exactly the wrong thing to do. Petting a dog when he's acting in a fearful manner actually serves as a reward for the behavior; it's almost as if we're telling the dog that being afraid in this situation is the right thing to do. Such

treatment actually makes the dog more likely to be afraid the next time.

For severe cases of fear and anxiety, there now exists a collection of veterinary pharmaceuticals to calm the dog and reduce its emotional state. However, for the average dog's fearfulness, ignoring the dog's anxiety and going about things normally is often the best way to blast through this emotional problem. For example, suppose your dog is afraid of thunder. If the dog has already had obedience classes, clipping a leash on him during a thunderstorm and practicing some of the simple exercises he has learned will help assure him that things are normal. Reward the dog with treats, petting, or praise—the way you did when you first trained him. The dog may at first appear puzzled by the fact that you're ignoring the state of affairs that is frightening him, but ultimately he will decide that if you—leader of the pack—are not bothered by the situation, then everything is all right and his fears are unfounded.

What Signs Indicate
That a Dog Is Aggressive?

T HAT FRIENDLY DOG that may be resting at your feet or on the sofa next to you has a dark and dangerous heritage. In their evolutionary past, dogs were predators that hunted and killed for a living, using a strong muzzle and a mouth full of teeth. Those same weapons could be used socially, to emphasize who was boss or had ownership of desirable goodies. Although we toned down dogs' aggressive tendencies when we domesticated them, some dogs can be provoked back into those primitive behavior patterns under certain circumstances.

Domestic dogs are bred well enough that they must have a good reason to bite before they resort to that behavior, and only a limited number of reasons trigger this response in dogs. First you must understand that the primary purpose of aggression in social situations is not to hurt and maim, but rather to change the behavior of another creature. For that reason, dogs clearly signal their aggressive intentions before acting. The idea is that the threat alone should be enough to change behavior, so actual biting occurs only if the aggressive signals are ignored. The signals indicating an aggressive threat include

- A prolonged direct stare
- Raised hackles
- Growling
- Showing the teeth
- Arching the body
- Walking stiffly
- Curling the tail between the legs or holding the tail very high over the back and fluffed out
- For dogs with pricked ears, having them lowered to the side to look like a wide "V" or airplane wings

Many dog owners might be surprised to see such behaviors in trivial situations, such as when the dog wants to keep possession of a pair of your socks or a plush toy. Such signs are easily missed in puppies, but the play growling and nipping that you think of as cute in a pup can escalate to a major problem as the dog matures. That's because once aggressive behaviors develop, they never disappear on their own. Dogs quickly learn that, by using aggression, they can get what they want or shield themselves in stressful situations. We

humans must solve the problem, but first we must recognize that it is aggression when the behavior occurs.

Before you go into a panic, it is important to ask just how serious the threat of being bitten by your dog actually is. If you believe the media reports, dog bites are an epidemic and more people die because their pet goes into a rage than are dying in foreign wars. Gathering statistics on dog bites is difficult, but one class of dog bites must, by law, be registered with the government—namely, those resulting in death. One scientific study looked at a period of nineteen years and found that there were 238 dog bite–related deaths in all of the United States during that time—an average of 12 per year. Compared to being bitten by a dog, you are nearly 8 times more likely to die by being struck by lightning (90 deaths per year), 26 times more likely to die by drowning in your bathtub (322 per year), 49 times more likely to die by drowning in a swimming pool (596 per year), and 66 times more likely to die when using your bicycle (795 per year). Apparently, dog bites are rather low on the list of common hazards.

Why, then, the media frenzy about "dangerous dogs"? A professor I know who teaches journalism (but doesn't want his name mentioned) explained it to me this way: "Good news doesn't sell. Do you think the headline 'Dog Makes Owner Smile and Feel Good' would sell papers? The rule that we teach aspiring journalists is 'If it bleeds, it leads,' and nowadays we add the reminder that 'dogs don't sue for defamation.'"

Are Some Dog Breeds
More Aggressive Than Others?

I S YOUR DOG potentially a lethal weapon? Every time the media report that someone has been mauled by a dog, this question arises in the minds of many people. Specifically, the public is now worrying about the possibility that certain dog breeds might be "bad" or at least potentially unsafe to keep in the city.

The reasoning goes that dogs have been bred for many purposes, and some, like Doberman Pinschers and German Shepherd Dogs, have been selected for watchdog and guarding services. Since these duties could require the dogs to bite people, the concern is that such animals might be predisposed to bite everybody.

Gathering statistics on dog bites is difficult. Many bites are innocuous, such as those that result from an overeager dog who punched a hole in your thumb when you offered him a treat. Others are more severe but may be treated at home. Of the bites that actually require medical treatment, many are not recorded in an accessible data bank and are thus lost to researchers. Even when bites are recorded, often the breed of dog involved is not identified.

Nevertheless, one agency, the US National Center for Injury Prevention and Control, has been looking at records of deaths due to dog bites collected over several decades, and it has found clear trends. Note, though, that the fact that a certain breed ranks high on a list of problem dogs may not be significant. Obviously, popular breeds will necessarily be represented in higher numbers for any given problem, so it is important to take into account how many dogs of a particular breed are around. It appears that, compared to their popularity, some breeds are significantly less likely to be involved in fatal dog bites. Leaving out the breeds that are simply too tiny to do fatal damage, the four breeds of dogs least likely to be involved in such incidents, although they have the bite strength to do so, are (beginning with the lowest proportional fatal bite frequency)

- Labrador Retriever
- Dachshunds
- Golden Retriever
- Bulldog

It may well be that the enduring popularity of Labrador Retrievers and Golden Retrievers as family pets is due in part to the fact that they are so safe.

However, the national data also shows that some dog breeds are more prone to kill, and pit bulls (defined here as American pit bull terriers, Staffordshire Bull Terriers, and American Staffordshire Terriers) are significantly overrepresented among dog breeds responsible for biting deaths. The national statistics on fatal dog bites indicate that the eight dog breeds (starting with the most dangerous) that account for the majority of these tragic cases of aggression are

1. Pit bulls and pit bull types
2. Rottweilers and Rottweiler crosses
3. Malamutes and Husky types
4. Wolf-dog hybrids
5. Chow Chows

6. Akitas
7. German Shepherd Dogs
8. Doberman Pinschers

This does not mean that every dog of these breeds is a born murderer, any more than we can guarantee that every dog in the least aggressive groups will not bite. All that the science gives us is probabilities; whether any specific Golden Retriever or Rottweiler is aggressive depends on who its owner is, how the dog was raised and socialized, and how it was trained and integrated into human society. There are kissy-faced Rottweilers and nasty Golden Retrievers in the world, and humans must take some responsibility for both the good and the bad outcomes.

While this research makes it clear that dog breeds do matter, the study also found that some other factors are important—such as the dog's sex and sexual status. Male dogs were 6.2 times more likely to fatally bite someone, and sexually intact dogs were 2.6 times more likely to be involved in attacks than neutered dogs were.

Who the victim is and what the victim does also play a role. Sadly, more than half of the victims of dog bites are children aged twelve or younger. However, the victims of many of these dog bites often play a part in precipitating the tragedy. In 53 percent of dog bite fatalities, there was some suggestion that the dog was provoked by being struck, being poked in the eye, having things thrown at it, or the like.

The behavior of the dog's owner is also important. Dogs who are chained or kept confined in a small yard are approximately three times more likely to fatally bite people. One important statistic that confirms owners' roles in their dogs' actions is that fully 88.8 percent of dogs that bite have never been given any obedience training.

Do Dogs Feel Jealousy and Envy?

JEALOUSY AND ENVY are common human emotions in social settings. You might say it's the art of counting the other person's blessings instead of your own. Some people believe that dogs don't feel such emotions. A different view came from a dog sled racer I met outside of Dawson City. He was getting ready to harness his team, and the dogs were milling around in a friendly, excited manner. I reached over to pet a handsome, blue-eyed Siberian Husky, but the racer warned me off, saying "If you pet one, you have to pet them all. They get really jealous. If they think that one of them is getting more of anything—affection, food, or whatever—they turn into green-eyed monsters."

In all social situations there are inequities, and some individuals come out better than others when it comes to rewards. Scientists tend to separate emotions into two categories: primary and secondary. "Primary emotions," such as fear, anger, disgust, joy, and surprise, are considered to be universal. "Secondary emotions," such as guilt, shame, jealousy, and envy, are thought to require more complex cognitive processes. For example, in the case of envy you have to actively pay attention to what the other individual is getting and compare it to what you're getting for your efforts. Although clear cases of jealousy and envy have been observed in primates, such as chimpanzees and baboons, the argument has been made that jealousy and envy would be unlikely emotions in an animal like the dog, because these emotions require self-awareness at a level that, until recently, was doubted in dogs. However, people who live around dogs often observe it in their pets.

One commonly observed manifestation of jealousy in dogs results because of the complex relationship between a mother dog, her puppies, and her owner. Unlike humans, a canine mother does not maintain the maternal instinct for her children all her life. As soon as the puppies are able to survive on their own, her maternal instinct for the current litter wanes, and it is certainly lost by the time she next goes into heat. Young puppies are, of course, very cute and cuddly, so it is natural for them to receive a lot of affection from the people in the house. More knowledgeable owners may try to treat all of the dogs with equal care and attention, but usually the effort is to no avail. The mother dog sees her owner's attention being diverted away from her toward the puppies, and she becomes

jealous. In response, she may begin ignoring the pups and trying to exclude them from the maternal nest. This behavior can escalate to the point where she might actually become aggressive toward the pups or even toward her owner.

It is strange that behavioral scientists often ignore such common observations. It is well accepted that dogs have a broad range of emotions. Dogs are certainly social animals, and jealousy and envy are triggered by social interactions. Dogs also have the same hormone, oxytocin, that has been shown to be involved in expressions of both love and jealousy in experiments involving humans.

Friederike Range of the University of Vienna, decided to see whether dogs show jealousy in an experimental situation in which two dogs perform the same task but one gets rewarded while the other does not. Each dog had learned the simple trick of "shaking hands" by extending a paw and putting it in a person's hand. For the test, the dogs were arranged in pairs, with the two dogs seated beside one another. Both dogs in each pair were individually commanded to "shake hands," but only one dog received a reward. It was expected that if dogs experience jealousy or envy, the unrewarded dog might respond to this unfair distribution of rewards by refusing to continue to obey the command. That is exactly what happened. The dog that was not getting treats for performing soon stopped doing the task. Furthermore, the dog that was not rewarded showed clear signs of stress or annoyance when its partner got the reward.

Some people might protest that this behavior does not really show jealousy. It may well be that the dog who was not being rewarded stopped responding simply because all unrewarded behaviors eventually tend to disappear, because of the process that learning theorists call "extinction." To make sure that it was the interaction between the dogs that was important, rather than just the frustration of not being rewarded, a similar experiment was conducted in which each dog performed the task without a partner but also without any reward. Under these circumstances, the dog continued to present its paw for a much longer time, and it did not show the same signs of frustration and annoyance.

One thing that emerged from these studies was the fact that jealousy and envy in dogs are not quite as complex as in human beings. When human beings are involved in competitive social situations, every aspect of the reward is carefully scrutinized to try to determine who is getting the best outcome. Dogs do not view this situation under the same kind of microscope. This difference became evident when the experimenters changed the situation in a subtle way.

Now, again, we have two dogs sitting in front of the experimenter, each being asked in turn to place a paw in the researcher's hand. Both dogs are being rewarded for this activity, but one dog gets a very desirable treat (a piece of sausage) while the other dog gets a less desirable treat (a piece of bread). In human beings, this scenario might be the equivalent of two corporate employees who perform equally well and are both given promotions but one is rewarded with a new, posh corner office, while the other gets a smaller, more austere office down the hall. Under such circumstances it is reasonable to expect the less favored individual to feel jealous and envious. In the case of the dogs, however, even though one is receiving a better reward than the other, both dogs continue to work, and they seem to be quite happy with the situation. This means that dogs are sensitive to "fairness" (whether everyone is being rewarded for their efforts) but not "equity" (whether all of the rewards are equal).

Can a Dog Really Suffer from Depression?

ALTHOUGH, AS WE'VE seen, dogs can feel the basic emotions, there is still a question as to whether dogs can suffer from psychological mood disorders that are characterized by extreme emotional states, such as depression.

It was the early 1980s when Nicholas Dodman of the Cummings School of Veterinary Medicine at Tufts University was standing next to a colleague watching a dog named Max that had been brought into the animal behavior clinic. Max had lost his appetite, was not eating or drinking the way he normally did, and thus was losing weight quickly. He seemed lethargic, spending a lot more time than usual sleeping. When he was awake he seemed nervous and edgy, and common events seemed to worry him. None of the activities that normally made him happy seemed to interest him. Any psychologist seeing a human being with Max's symptoms would conclude that he was probably suffering from depression. However, when Dodman concluded that the dog was depressed and anxious, his colleague shook his head and warned him about the dangers of treating dogs as if they had such humanlike feelings. He argued, "Dogs don't experience the same mental states and emotions that people do."

Dodman's colleague was really restating one of the beliefs of many scientists, which is that only humans have feelings and conscious mental processes. Charles Darwin, whose theory of evolution transformed our view of the biological world, was the first to challenge this viewpoint. Darwin suggested that the emotional experiences of animals are similar to those of humans, but they might not be as complex or varied.

Dodman was clearly siding with Darwin when he answered his colleague by saying, "Well, how about this? Let's give the dog an antidepression drug and see what happens." What happened made history because the dog's behavior improved dramatically. At the biological level of analysis, this is what should have happened, since the brain and neurochemistry of the dog are very similar to those of humans.

Today, most veterinarians are trained to accept that animals have emotions and can suffer from some of the same emotional problems that people do. Such problems include not only depression, but also anxiety, irrational fears and phobias, obsessive and compulsive behaviors, and a broad range of neurotic and stress-related problems. Currently, there is a growing field of research called *Animal Behavioral Pharmacology* and most veterinarians have

been trained in using psychologically active drugs. Drugs for pets are now big business, prompting Pfizer, one of the largest pharmaceutical companies in the world, to establish a companion animal division, which earned the company nearly a billion dollars last year.

How widespread such emotional conditions are in pets is difficult to determine. However, Sainsbury's Pet Insurance in the United Kingdom has been collecting some information. Sainsbury's suggests that depression and anxiety are widespread in the British canine population; the report indicated that 623,000 UK dogs and cats had suffered mentally in the previous year, while more than 900,000 suffered loss of appetite because of stress or emotional problems.

Deficits in serotonin, a hormone that serves as a neurotransmitter in the brain, seem to play an important role in triggering depression. However, environmental conditions, such as loss or separation from an owner or a companion dog, moving to a new location, trauma from injury, disease or abuse, or being tied out on a tether and socially isolated for long periods, can also trigger depression in dogs.

When faced with psychological problems in dogs, veterinarians like Dodman turned to the drugs designed for people. Just as Dodman had predicted, Prozac in various forms successfully controlled depression and anxiety-related problems in dogs. This finding prompted Lilly, the pharmaceutical company that introduced Prozac, to create a chewable beef-flavored version of the medication specifically designed for use by dogs.

As with humans, certain behavioral treatments can also combat depression. Increased exercise, which helps depressed people, also helps depressed dogs. Increased social interaction and play, and perhaps the addition of another dog to the family to provide continued or renewed social support and companionship, can often improve the dog's condition dramatically.

Can Dogs Laugh?

IN THE MINDS of most people, the equivalent of a dog smiling is when he's wagging his tail. However, there is actually one canine facial expression that comes close to what we mean by smiling in humans. In this expression, slightly opened jaws reveal the dog's tongue lapping out over his front teeth. Frequently the eyes take on a teardrop shape at the same time, as if being pulled upward slightly at the outer corners. It is a casual expression that is usually seen when the dog is relaxed, playing, or interacting socially (especially with people). The moment any anxiety or stress is introduced into the situation, the dog's mouth closes and you can no longer see the tongue.

This expression, with the tongue lolling forward, has actually been recognized for a long time as representing a smile. For example, we find children's toys dating back to the time of the pharaohs of Egypt that consist of the figure of a dog on a little platform with wheels. It is designed to be attached to a string and pulled across the floor. The face of the dog, however, has an exaggerated large tongue lapping out over his front teeth and hanging down. The translation of this toy's name is "the smiling dog."

Even if we believe that dogs actually smile, there is still the question of whether they can ratchet their emotional expression up a notch and produce something that is the canine equivalent of laughter. Animal behavior researchers used to believe that laughter was an emotional expression found only in humans. However, the Nobel Prize–winning ethologist Konrad Lorenz suggested that dogs are capable of laughing and they do so when they're playing. Canine laughter begins with the doggy equivalent of smiling (namely, the slightly opened jaws revealing the tongue over the front teeth) but also includes a sound that is much like panting.

Patricia Simonet at Sierra Nevada College recorded those panting-laughter sounds while dogs played. On analyzing the recordings, she found that they involved a broader range of frequencies than does regular dog panting. In one experiment, Simonet noticed that puppies romped for joy when they heard recordings of these sounds; and in another, she was able to show that these same sounds helped to calm dogs in an animal shelter.

Humans can imitate these sounds, but it takes some "tuning." My first attempts were not very successful, causing virtually no response or at best puzzled looks from my dogs. However, I was eventually able to shape a set of sounds that reliably evoked their interest. It required conscious monitoring of my mouth shape to get the sound pattern right. For me, what seems to work the best is something like "hhuh-hhah-hhuh-hhah . . ." with the "hhuh" sound made with slightly rounded lips, while the "hhah" sound is made with a sort of open-mouthed smiling expression. The sound has to be breathy with no actual voicing, meaning that if you touch your throat while making this sound, you should not feel any vibration. When I make these sounds, my

dogs sit up and wag their tails as they approach me from across the room.

After those informal experiments, I extended my observations and have been able to use my human imitation of dog laughter sounds to calm worried, anxious, and shy dogs in a dog obedience class and in other settings. It seems to help if you glance at the dog directly only for brief intervals, alternating with glancing away. In addition, short, quick side-to-side head movements sometimes appear to improve the effect. The technique seems to work best in calming dogs that are moderately anxious or insecure. If the negative emotions experienced by the dog are too intense, however, it does not seem to help.

Do Dogs Know Mathematics?

SOME PEOPLE DOUBT that dogs are capable of even the most rudimentary form of quantitative thinking. The most basic form of analyzing the world in a quantitative way is judging size—namely, answering the question of whether one thing is larger than another. Early researchers would present dogs with two balls of hamburger— one large and one small—and when they found that dogs were as likely to choose the small one as the large one, they concluded that dogs could not estimate size. However, this test is flawed. Dogs think in an opportunistic manner—a sort of "a bird in the hand is worth two in the bush" mentality. If the two hamburger balls were at different distances, the dog would always grab the closer one, but if they were at equal distances, the dog would go after the larger one, showing that it understood the notion of size.

Norton Milgram, at the University of Toronto, confirmed that dogs can judge size well by presenting dogs with a tray containing two objects of different sizes. If the dog pushed the correct object, underneath the object the dog would find a food treat. Both objects had been rubbed with the treat so that scent could not serve as a hint, and the dog had to rely on his visual estimates of size. In this scenario, dogs can be taught always to pick the larger (or smaller) of two objects, regardless of the shape or identity of the objects, and they learn this distinction fairly easily.

A slightly more difficult aspect of quantitative reasoning is the judgment of numerosity. Simply put, "numerosity" is the ability to compare the number of items in two different groups. We do this when we judge which of two crowds contains more people, and we can do it without counting or having any idea of the specific number of people in either group. Thus, a dog who runs to a pile containing ten pieces of kibble, rather than to the pile next to it that contains only two pieces of kibble, may have based that decision on his judgment of the number of kibble bits in each pile. In the laboratory, dogs prove that they can judge numerosity by learning to press a panel that has more (or fewer) dots painted on it for a food reward.

The next level up is simple counting, an ability that dogs frequently demonstrate, especially working and sporting dogs. For example, in field trials with retrievers, to successfully complete the higher-level tasks the dog must be able to count to at least 3. The reason for this requirement is that if three ducks have been dropped and the dog has already retrieved two, the dog must know that there is still one more out in the field to retrieve.

If dogs can count, it seems natural to ask whether they can do simple arithmetic. Robert Young of the Pontifical Catholic University in Brazil, and Rebecca West of the University of Lincoln in the United Kingdom, attempted to investigate this idea by modifying a test used to prove that human infants have the ability to count. The procedure involves something called "preferential viewing," which simply measures the amount of time that infants spend looking at things. Research confirms that infants (just like adults) will stare at something unexpected or unusual for a longer time.

The human test for counting is quite simple. First the child is a shown a small doll on a table, and then a low screen is put in front of the doll to block the child's view. While the child watches,

the experimenter shows another doll to the child and then puts it behind the screen. If able to count, the child should expect to see two dolls when the screen is raised—and sometimes the child does. However, sometimes the experimenter secretly removes one of the dolls so that now when the screen is raised, only one doll is visible. In this case, the babies stare at what is on the table for much longer after the screen has been raised. Psychologists believe that this finding confirms that infants have made the mental calculation and are now surprised to find that the number of dolls they're seeing is different from what they expected.

In the canine version of this test, the dog was shown a single large treat and a low screen was put in front of it. Then the dog watched as the experimenter obviously placed another treat behind the screen. If the dog could do the math, he would know that $1 + 1 = 2$ and he would expect to see two treats when the screen was raised.

However, just as with the babies, sometimes the experimenters surreptitiously removed the second treat so that when the screen was raised the dog saw only one. Also as with the babies, the dogs stared at this unexpected outcome for a longer time than they did when the arithmetic came out correctly, apparently "surprised" at what they saw. Similarly, if an extra treat was secretly added, so that the dogs saw three instead of the expected two, the dogs appear to be equally surprised. These observations suggest that dogs not only can count, but also can do simple addition and subtraction.

The ability to count and do simple arithmetic might seem to be a superfluous skill for dogs, but it is a useful ability that would have been vital to dog's wild ancestors. For example, it is useful for a female to know whether all of her pups are present in the den or if one of them has somehow gone astray and she should launch a search-and-rescue mission.

Do Dogs Have a Sense of Music?

MANY PEOPLE BELIEVE that a dog's howl is a canine attempt to make music, because dogs sometimes howl when music is played or sung. Compared to wild canines, domestic dogs bark a lot more and howl only occasionally. Howling is a form of communication that can indicate loneliness in an isolated dog, but it often serves other social functions. Wolves howl to assemble the pack and to reinforce the identity of the group. Upon hearing the howling, group members gather together and join in the song of their pack. Once the howling begins, it often turns into a joyous celebration—the dogs or wolves happily announcing their own presence and their camaraderie with others of their species in what might be termed a spontaneous canine jam session.

The kind of human music that most often induces a dog to howl is produced on wind instruments, particularly reed instruments, such as clarinets or saxophones. Sometimes dogs can be induced to howl by a long note on the violin or even by a human holding a long note while singing. Perhaps these sounds resemble proper howls to the listening dog and it feels the need to answer and join the chorus.

There are, however, reports of dogs with definite tastes in music and some sense of what constitutes good music. A Bulldog named Dan was owned by Dr. George Robinson Sinclair, the organist at Hereford Cathedral in London. Sinclair was a friend of Sir Edward William Elgar, best known for writing *Pomp and Circumstance* and *Land of Hope and Glory*. Elgar developed a fondness for Dan because he felt that the dog had a good sense of musical quality. Dan would frequently attend choir practices with his master, and he would growl at choristers who sang out of tune, thereby greatly endearing himself to the composer.

Eventually Elgar ended up writing a musical tribute to the dog. It came about this way. Dan, like many other Bulldogs, had a dislike of being in water. One day, on a walk along the banks of the River Wye, Dan fell in. As quickly as he could, he scrambled out and vigorously shook himself, soaking both Sinclair and Elgar. Greatly amused by this incident, Sinclair challenged Elgar to put it to music. Elgar took up the challenge and immediately began his musical interpretation. It later became one of the *Enigma Variations* (number 11), thus musically immortalizing a dog that had a sense of when people were singing in tune or not.

Richard Wilhelm Wagner, best known as the composer of the series of four operas that make up the *Ring Cycle*, had a strong appreciation of the musical taste of dogs. He provided a special stool in his study for Peps, his Cavalier King Charles Spaniel. As Wagner composed, he would play the piano or sing passages that he was working on. The composer kept his eyes on the dog and modified musical phrases in response to how the dog reacted. Wagner noticed that Peps responded differently to melodies depending on their musical keys. Certain passages in one key might cause an occasional calm tail wag, while passages in other keys might arouse an excited response. This phenomenon put the germ of an idea in Wagner's mind that ultimately led him to a device called the "musical motif."

Motifs associate specific musical keys with particular moods or emotions in the operatic drama. For example, in the opera *Tannhäuser* the key of E-flat major is linked with the concept of holy love and salvation, while E major is tied to the notion of sensual love and debauchery. In all of his subsequent operas, Wagner came to use musical motifs to identify important characters and other aspects of the drama. When Peps died, Wagner was devastated and found it difficult to apply his mind to composing until he obtained another dog (of the same breed). This new dog, Fips, soon took his place on a specially upholstered stool situated next to Wagner's piano, so that he could render his canine musical expertise and criticism as needed.

Research confirms that dogs have musical preferences and react differently to particular types of music. Psychologist Deborah Wells at Queens University in Belfast exposed dogs in an animal shelter to different types of music. The dogs' behaviors were observed when they listened to either a compilation of popular music (including Britney Spears, Robbie Williams, and Bob Marley), classical music (including Grieg's *Morning*, Vivaldi's *Four Seasons*, and Beethoven's *Ode to Joy*), or recordings by heavy-metal rock bands such as Metallica. To see whether the dogs were really responding to the musical aspects of the sounds, they were also exposed to recordings of human conversation and a period of quiet.

The kind of music that the dogs listened to made a difference. When the researchers played heavy-metal music, the dogs became quite agitated and began barking. Listening to popular music or human conversation did not produce behaviors that were noticeably different from having no sound at all. Classical music, on the other hand, seemed to have a calming effect on the dogs. While listening to it, their level of barking was significantly reduced, and the dogs often lay down and settled in place. Wells summarized her findings by saying, "It is well established that music can influence our moods. Classical music, for example, can help to reduce levels of stress, whilst grunge music can promote hostility, sadness, tension and fatigue. It is now believed that dogs may be as discerning as humans when it comes to musical preference."

Do Dogs Have ESP Abilities?

MANY PEOPLE BELIEVE that dogs have psychic abilities of various sorts, such as the ability to predict the impending death of a person, or to sense spirits or ghosts, or to have a psychic link of some sort with a beloved master that is attuned to the master's welfare. In recent years this issue attracted the interest of scientists because of some research done by Rupert Sheldrake, who holds a PhD in biochemistry. Sheldrake argued that "the most convincing evidence for telepathy between people and animals comes from the study of dogs that know when their owners are coming home. This anticipatory behavior is common. Many dog owners take it for granted without reflecting on its wider implications." Sheldrake has collected more than five hundred cases in which dogs appear to anticipate an owner's arrival. Furthermore, he claims that this phenomenon is not due to an innate ability to tell time, because the dogs seem to foresee these events even when the time is not regular or predictable. And it can't be that their sensitive ears are picking up the sound of a familiar vehicle, since they anticipate the owner's return even if the person comes by foot or via bus or taxi.

Sheldrake describes the striking case of Carole Bartlett, who lives in Chiselhurst in Kent, England. She often leaves Sam (a Lab-

rador Retriever–Greyhound mix) with her husband when she goes to the theater or to visit friends in London. To return home requires a twenty-five-minute train journey and then a five-minute walk from the station. Carole's husband does not know which train she will return on, and she might arrive at any time between six and eleven o'clock at night. Sheldrake quotes Carole as saying, "My husband says Sam comes downstairs off my bed (where he spends the day when I go out) to wait at the front door half an hour before my return." The reason this report appears so remarkable is that the dog seems to begin waiting for Carole at about the time she's just starting her journey home, when she is still many miles and thirty minutes away from her front door.

The most closely studied case of supposed canine ESP involves a mixed-breed terrier named Jaytee, owned by Pamela Smart of Rams-bottom, England. As with Carole Bartlett's Sam, Jaytee seemed to anticipate Pam's return by running to the window or outside to sit on the porch just about the time that his mistress was beginning her return trip home. This anticipation occurred even when Pam's schedule was irregular and her travel times were unknown by other members of her family. In an attempt to verify Jaytee's telepathic abilities, the Austrian State Television network sent two film crews. One crew followed Pam as she walked around the downtown area, and the other stayed at home and continually filmed Jaytee. After a couple of hours, Pam and her crew decided to head home, and at that very moment Jaytee went out on the porch and remained there until Pam returned. The results of this experiment received a lot of media attention, with television commentators describing the dog as "psychic" and "always correct in his anticipations."

Richard Wiseman, a psychologist at the University of Hertford-shire, followed up on this study with additional tests of Jaytee's telepathy. His first task was to eliminate any possible nontelepathic clues that might trigger the dog's behavior. This meant that Pam could not leave and return at a familiar, expected time, or use a car whose sound was familiar and might be picked up at a distance. Specifically, Wiseman's team took Pam to a remote location and used a special calculator to generate a random time for her return. Pam was told that they were going to return home only a few seconds before the group actually started back. Meanwhile, another member of the research team remained at Pam's home and made a complete video record of Jaytee's behavior.

What the researchers found was that Jaytee was an extremely vigilant dog, typically running to the window or out on the porch more than a dozen times during any of Pam's absences. Sometimes an event such as a person walking by or a car pulling up to the curb was the obvious reason for his investigation. Sometimes, however, there was no apparent reason for Jaytee's going to the window. Unfortunately, the majority of these "unexplained" trips to the window did not coincide all that closely with the times that Pam started home. In a subsequent interview, Wiseman summarized his results, saying, "At a randomly selected time the owner returned home and yes indeed the dog was at the window at that point. When we rolled back the film and looked at the rest of it we found the dog was constantly going to the window. In fact, it was at the window so much it would be more surprising if it wasn't at the window when the owner was returning home!"

So why were Pam and her family so sure that Jaytee was able to accurately predict her return? Their certainty likely has to do with some well-known thinking biases that human beings have. These involve a kind of selective memory based on what psychologists call "confirmation bias." Confirmation bias is a mode of thinking in which people tend to notice, or even look for, events that confirm their beliefs, and to ignore or perhaps undervalue the relevance of observations that contradict their beliefs. The classic example is people who believe they have a system to beat various games at casinos. Such individuals tend to remember only the nights they won significant amounts of money using that method, and to forget the nights they lost, perhaps explaining that on those nights they didn't follow the system perfectly. Obviously, such skewed memory would, over time, produce an unjustifiable belief in the relationship between winning and their system. Similar thinking and selective remembering can result in the belief in a dog's telepathic ability to detect when its owner is starting homeward.

Do Dogs Dream?

MANY PEOPLE BELIEVE that dogs do dream. Most dog owners have noticed that at various times during their sleep,
some dogs may quiver, make leg twitches, or even growl or snap at
a sleep-created phantom, giving the impression that they're dreaming about something. At the structural level, the brains of dogs are
similar to those of humans. In addition, during sleep the brain wave
patterns of dogs are similar to those of people, and they exhibit the
same stages of electrical activity that are observed in humans—all
of which is consistent with the idea that dogs are dreaming.

Actually, it would be more surprising if dogs didn't dream, since
recent evidence suggests that animals that are simpler and less
intelligent than dogs seem to dream. Matthew Wilson and Kenway
Louie of the Massachusetts Institute of Technology report that the
brains of sleeping rats function in a way that irresistibly suggests
dreaming. Much of the dreaming you do at night is associated with
the activities you engaged in that day. The same seems to be the case
in rats. Thus, a rat that ran a complex maze during the day might be
expected to dream about it at night. From electrical recordings of
the rat hippocampus (an area of the brain associated with memory
formation and storage) made while the rats were awake and learning

a maze, Wilson and Louie found that some electrical patterns were quite specific and identifiable, depending on what the rat was doing. Later, when the rats were asleep and their brain waves indicated that they had entered the stage in which humans normally dream, these same patterns of brain waves appeared. In fact, the patterns were so clear and specific that the researchers were able to tell where in the maze the rat would be if it were awake, and whether it would be moving or standing still. Wilson cautiously described the results, saying, "The animal is certainly recalling memories of those events as they occurred during the awake state, and it is doing so during dream sleep and that's just what people do when they dream."

Since a dog's brain is more complex than the rat's and shows the same electrical sequences, it is reasonable to assume that dogs are dreaming as well. There is also evidence that they dream about common dog activities. This kind of research takes advantage of the fact that the brainstem (the pons) contains a special structure that keeps all of us from acting out our dreams. When scientists removed or inactivated the part of the brain that suppresses acting out of dreams in dogs, they observed that the dogs began to move around,

even though electrical recordings of the dogs' brains indicated that they were still fast asleep. The dogs started to move only when the brain entered that stage of sleep associated with dreaming. During the course of a dream episode, these dogs actually began to execute the actions that they were performing in their dreams. For example, researchers found that a dreaming pointer may immediately start searching for game and may even go on point, a sleeping Springer Spaniel may flush an imaginary bird in its dreams, while a dreaming Doberman Pinscher may pick a fight with a dream burglar.

It is really quite easy to determine when your dog is dreaming without resorting to brain surgery or electrical recordings. All you have to do is to watch the dog from the time he starts to doze off. As the dog's sleep deepens, his breathing will become more regular. After about 20 minutes for an average-sized dog, the first dream should start. You will recognize the change because the dog's breathing will become shallow and irregular. There may be odd muscle twitches, and you can even see the dog's eyes moving behind closed eyelids if you look closely enough. The eyes are moving because the dog is actually looking at the dream images as if they were real images of the world. These eye movements are most characteristic of dreaming sleep. When human beings are awakened during this rapid eye movement (or REM) sleep phase, they virtually always report that they were dreaming.

Not all dogs dream the same way. It is an odd fact that small dogs have more dreams than big dogs. A dog as small as a Toy Poodle may dream once every ten minutes, while a dog as large as a Mastiff or a Great Dane may have about an hour between dreams. The difference is that the big dog's dreams last longer.

Can You Make Your Dog More Intelligent?

I T IS POSSIBLE to increase the intelligence of your dog. Although it may be hard to believe, you can actually change the physiology of your dog's brain. You can make it larger and more efficient simply by providing certain experiences for your pet. The same process will make your dog more intelligent and give his personality an added degree of stress resistance.

The research supporting these startling claims began in the 1940s when Canadian psychologist Donald O. Hebb took home a few lab rats and gave them to his children to keep as pets. The children played with these animals and let them run around and explore much of Hebb's family home. Obviously, the life these rats were leading, and the environments they were being allowed to explore, were much more complex and stimulating than the standard barren laboratory cage, which might include only some wood shavings to rest on, a water bottle, and a food tray. When these animals were later tested on their ability to learn complex mazes (the rat equivalent of an intelligence test), they proved to be much smarter than their littermates that had been raised in boring cages where they had little to do or explore and where there were no problems or interesting situations to exercise their minds.

Shortly after this first set of tests on the pet rats, some of Hebb's research associates repeated these experiments using dogs. They compared the learning ability of dogs reared as pets (who received all of the stimulation and varied experiences that a typical family dog normally has) with that of dogs reared in the usual barren kennels in the lab. They found that the dogs reared in the more complex home environment not only learned faster, but seemed to be less fearful and considerably less stressed in the testing situations.

Over the years, researchers have proven that these behavioral changes are the result of transformations in the physiology of the brain. The brains of animals that have lived in changing and complex environments actually become larger. New connections develop between existing neurons in the cortex as a result of experience. Recent studies have demonstrated that it is even possible to grow new neural cells in important areas of the brain that are associated with learning, memory, and the organization of behavior.

The crucial aspect of an animal's experience that causes these positive changes in its brain is exposure to a wide variety of interesting places and things. The best results come when this exposure is combined with frequent opportunities to learn new things, solve problems, and freely investigate, manipulate, and interact with objects and environmental features. The data unambiguously shows that such experience leads to individuals who not only tend to be more inquisitive and more able to learn quickly and perform complex tasks, but also are less fearful and emotional.

Recent research by psychologist Norton W. Milgram and his associates at the University of Toronto showed that the benefits of such experiences are not restricted to growing puppies. Not only do adults and even elderly animals benefit from having richer environments, but their problem-solving experiences seem to help offset the usual decline in mental efficiency that is seen in older dogs.

For those of us who want to give our pet dog the advantage of a more efficient brain, the trick is simply to keep the dog's mind active, exposing him to new experiences, giving him new things to learn and puzzles to work out. Some different experiences can come out of just taking the dog to new places and on different routes on daily walks, or including the dog on day trips or when out doing various chores. However, a little bit of effort to pose problems that your dog must solve will work even better.

For most dogs, using food as the reward for solving problems and finding things will keep the dog's motivation high. For example, a number of different dog toys can be filled with kibble. When the object is rolled around or knocked about, it will dispense bits of kibble. If you're willing to put up with a bit of controlled destruction, you can put kibble or treats inside a cardboard box, old towel or rag, or crumpled plastic jugs and let the dog tear the item apart to get to the food inside. The cardboard rolls that toilet paper and paper towels come on are great for this. Put some kibble in them, crumple the ends, and let the pup tear apart the "toy" to get to the food. Many dog toys have cavities or pocket-like spaces, such as Kongs and hollow nylon bones. These provide places that can be filled with dog biscuits, peanut butter, cheese, or the like. The dog has to work at getting the food out. If you moisten some kibble, stuff the toy, and then freeze it, by the next day you will have a food-stuffed toy that the dog will have to work at for quite a while to get at the snack that he wants.

One variation on this theme is to turn meals into searches. Simply divide the dog's meal into small portions, each in a plastic container. Now hide them around the house and let the dog search for them. At first you will have to make the hiding places fairly obvious, but later you can make finding the next portion of dinner more of a challenge.

Actually, all forms of games based on hide and seek are good. If you have someone help you (I find visiting grandchildren are great for this), one person can hide and the other then encourages the dog to go find the person who is now out of sight. It helps if you give a command to direct the dog, like "Find Becky." In the beginning, the person who is hiding might have to actually call the dog from her place of concealment. Once the hidden person is found, the dog either gets a treat or gets a toy to play with. You can even play a form of "canine tennis," with the dog serving as the ball, by then sending the dog back to find the first person (who has now moved to a new place) and then sending the dog back to the second person (who has also moved) and so forth.

If your dog spends time outside, you should recognize that the average yard is usually a fairly boring and barren environment, except for interesting things that might pass nearby on the other side of the fence. You can make this environment a bit more stimulating by hanging ropes or inner tubes from a branch or from another elevated item in the yard for the dog to tug at. Change the terrain a bit by adding some big boxes that can serve as tunnels or platforms for the dog to run through or climb on. Small logs and lengths of PVC pipe (perhaps 5 inches, or about 13 centimeters, in diameter) can be laid down for the dog to walk and jump over while playing. If you have more than one dog, some barriers to hide behind or enclosures to hide in are useful, and the dogs will often create their own games using them. A child's wading pool with some water or sand can provide some additional chances for play and interaction. Frequently changing things in the yard will also provide stimulation.

Generally speaking, however, dogs are apt to find the environment inside the house, where people are moving about, more exciting than the average yard. Therefore, if you want the dog outside, you should go out there to play with him occasionally. Remember, you're not only building your relationship with your dog, but actually building him a better brain.

PART 3

How Do Dogs Communicate?

What Are Dogs Trying to Say
When They Bark?

F OR HUMANS, LANGUAGE sounds are fairly arbitrary. No set of word sounds has a common meaning for all members of our species. Many different sounds, in different languages, can mean the same thing. The words "perro," "chien," "Hund," and "dog" all mean the same thing, but there is virtually nothing in common among the sound patterns that make up these words. The sounds that animals use to communicate with each other, however, have much more uniformity. These sounds are different for different species, but (except for certain regional "dialects" among birds) within any one class of animals there seems to be some sort of fairly common or universal language, and a universally understood set of sound signals. The sounds in this code have three dimensions: pitch, duration, and frequency (repetition rate).

- *The meaning of pitch:* Low-pitched sounds (such as a dog's growl) usually indicate threat, anger, and the possibility of aggression. These sounds are interpreted as meaning "Stay away from me." High-pitched sounds mean the opposite, asking to be allowed to come closer or saying that it is safe to approach. The question is, why should

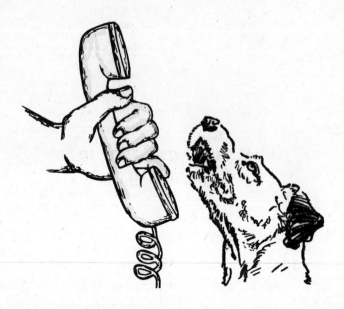

dogs use and understand this law of pitch? The answer
begins with the simple observation that big things
make low sounds. For example, take two empty water
tumblers—one large and one small—and tap each with
a spoon. The large one gives a lower-pitched ringing
sound. Obviously, a dog does not change his size simply
by changing the pitch of his sound signals. So why would
the receiver of this signal respond to these pitch variations at all, since they often do not represent the physical
reality? Now here is where evolution and the development of communication begin to weave their magic. Suppose you're an animal sending signals to those around
you. Since you know that other animals are paying attention to the pitch of your signals, you can now deliberately
use pitch variation as a means of communication. If you
wanted to make another animal move away or stay out of
your territory, you could send a low-pitched signal, like a

growl, suggesting that you're large and dangerous. Conversely, you could use a high-pitched signal, like a whimper, to suggest that you're rather small and therefore it is quite safe to approach you. Similarly, even if you're large, if you wished to signal that you intend no threat or harm when you approach another animal, you could whimper or whine to indicate that you intend to act like a small, harmless creature.

- *The meaning of duration:* Generally speaking, the longer the sound is, the more likely it is that the dog has made a conscious decision about the nature of the signal and his next behaviors. The threatening growl of a dominant dog that has every intention of holding his ground and not backing down will be both low-pitched and also long and sustained. A growl issued in shorter bursts indicates an element of fear, and that the dog is worried about whether it can successfully deal with an attack.

- *The meaning of frequency:* Sounds that are repeated often, at a fast rate, indicate a degree of excitement and urgency. Sounds that are spaced out, or not repeated, usually indicate a lower level of excitement. A dog giving an occasional bark or two at the window is showing only mild interest in something. A dog barking in multiple bursts and repeating them many times a minute is signaling that he feels that the situation is important and perhaps even a potential crisis.

Barking is an alarm sound. A barking dog is not threatening aggression unless the barking is pitched lower and mixed with growls. Let's consider how the most common types of barking should be interpreted.

- *A rapid string of two to four barks with pauses between bursts* is the most common form of barking. It is the classic alarm bark, meaning something like, "Call the pack. There's something going on that should be checked out."

- *Barking in a fairly continuous string but at a lower pitch and slower than the usual alarm bark* suggests that the dog is sensing an imminent problem. This sound means, "An intruder (or danger) is very close. I don't think he's friendly. Get ready to defend yourself!"

- *One or two sharp, short barks of high or midrange pitch* is the most typical greeting sound, and it usually replaces the alarm barks when the visitor is recognized as friendly. Many people are greeted in this way when they walk in the door. The message is "Hello there!" and is usually followed with the dog's typical greeting ritual.

- *A long string of solitary barks with deliberate pauses between each one* is a sign of a lonely dog asking for companionship.

- *A stutter bark, which sounds something like "Harr—ruff"* is usually given with front legs flat on the ground and the rear held high. It means simply, "Let's play!"

Why Do Dogs Bark,
and What Can We Do about It?

ONE OF THE most common complaints that people have about their dog is that it barks too much, but one of the reasons why humans and dogs formed their working relationship is probably the very fact that dogs bark. It all started in the dim past, when dogs began hanging around human settlements because primitive humans were slobs who would scatter garbage outside their camps. For dogs, that garbage was a free meal that didn't require hunting. The presence of the dogs was tolerated by our ancestors simply because the dogs would dispose of the refuse, thus keeping the smell and vermin level down.

Humans soon learned that there was another benefit to having dogs around, in that the dogs would sound the alarm when dangerous animals or potentially hostile strangers approached the settlement. Since the dogs were always vigilant, human guards did not need to be posted throughout the night, thus allowing for more rest and a better lifestyle. It takes only a short journey to get from dogs guarding the edge of the village to a dog living indoors and guarding an individual's home. Soon the dog's bark would serve the benign purpose of alerting the family to the approach of visitors (a sort of canine doorbell) or to warn of the approach of a potential thief (a canine burglar alarm). It seems obvious that for personal and community security purposes, the most effective dog is one with a loud and persistent bark. For this reason, a dog that barked loudly was kept and bred with others that also barked. One that did not bark was simply disposed of as being useless. In effect, one of the distinctions between wild canines and domestic dogs is that our domestic dogs bark, while wild dogs seldom do.

The main reason people have problems with barking is that they don't understand why the dog barks and what he expects you to do in response to his behavior. The most common form of barking is designed to sound the alarm or alert the pack. It really means something like, "Rally around me and check this out! There may be a problem here!" It consists of bursts of two or three barks with a short interval between them, something like "woof woof . . . woof woof woof . . . woof woof." The dog simply wants the leader of the pack and the other pack members to observe what he has detected and make a decision as to the proper course of action. Unfortunately, when

people are at home and such barking occurs, their typical response is something like, "Be quiet! . . . Stop that noise! . . . Shut up!"—which is a bad move. This sort of response indicates that the dog's master simply does not understand the basics of dog language. To a dog, loud, short utterances like "No!" "Shut up!" "Don't bark!" and so forth are interpreted as barks. Think of it this way: The dog barks to signal a potential problem. Now you (who are supposed to be the leader of the dog's pack) come over and also bark. This response clearly indicates that you agree this is the right time to sound the alarm, and it will often lead to more frantic barking on the part of the dog.

The appropriate response is to recognize the message that the dog is trying to send to you and to acknowledge it. The best thing to do is get up and check the window or the door that the dog is barking at in an obvious manner, so that the dog knows what you're doing. Remember, sometimes the dog is correct and there is something you need to respond to, but if it's a false alarm, such as a car pulling up to the curb or a delivery next door, simply reassure the dog with a calm phrase like "Good guarding, but we're quite safe." Give the dog a pat, lead him away from the door, and have him lie down next to you. In most cases, this is all that's needed. This approach works because the dog is asking for the leader of the pack to check out what might be a problem, and once this has been done and he is reassured that there is no danger, there's no need to continue alerting the household with his barking.

Remember that we specifically bred dogs to bark, so if your dog sounds the alarm at the approach of a stranger, or even at the sight of a cat outside your window, don't correct him. If there's no cause for action, just call the dog to your side and give him a quick pet or a rub. By barking, your dog is only doing the job that we designed dogs to do thousands of years ago.

What Does a Wagging Tail Mean?

PERHAPS THE MOST common misinterpretation of dog behavior is based on the myth that a dog who is wagging his tail is happy and friendly. While some tail wags are associated with happiness, others can signal a variety of quite different things, including fear and insecurity, social challenge, or even the warning that if you continue your approach you're apt to be bitten.

In some ways, tail wagging serves the same communication functions as a human smile, a polite greeting, or a nod of recognition. Smiles, for example, are social signals, and humans reserve most of their smiles for social situations, where somebody is present to see them. For dogs, the tail wag seems to have the same properties. A dog reserves tail wagging for things that are alive, such as a person, another dog, a cat, a horse, or perhaps a ball of lint that is moved by a breeze and might be alive. A dog that is alone will not wag its tail at any lifeless thing. If you put a bowl of its food down, the dog will wag its tail to express its gratitude to you. In contrast, when the dog walks into a room and finds its bowl full, it will approach and eat the food just as happily, but with no tail wagging other than, perhaps, a slight excitement tremor. This difference is one indication that tail wagging is meant as communication or language. In the same way that we don't talk to walls, dogs do not wag their tails to things that are not apparently alive.

If tail wags are language, then we need to know their vocabulary and grammar. The two major sources of information are the tail's position and its pattern of movement. Movement is a very important aspect of the signal, since dogs' eyes are much more sensitive to movement than they are to details or colors, so a moving tail is very visible to other dogs. Evolution has used a few additional tricks to make the tails even more visible, such as marking the tip of the tail with a light or dark color, making the underside of the tail lighter, or making the tail bushy.

The tail's position, specifically the height that it is held, can be viewed as a sort of emotional meter. If the tail is held at a middle height, the dog is relaxed. If the tail is held horizontally, the dog is attentive and alert. As the tail position moves up, it is a sign that the dog is becoming more threatening, with a vertical tail being a clearly dominant signal meaning, "I'm boss around here," or even a warn-

ing to "Back off or suffer the consequences." A lower tail position is a sign that the dog is being more submissive, is worried, or is feeling poorly. The extreme is the tail tucked under the body, which is a sign of fear and a request that says, "Please don't hurt me."

In the same way that there are different dialects in human languages, such as a southern drawl or a Maritime or New England twang, there are dialects in dogs' tail language. Different breeds carry their tails at different heights, from the nearly erect natural position common to Beagles and many terriers, to the low-slung tail of Greyhounds and Whippets. This means that all tail positions should be read relative to the average position that a dog normally holds its tail.

The movements that the tail makes give additional meaning to the signals. The speed of the wag indicates how excited the dog is, and it is independent of how broad the movements are. The size of each tail sweep tells us whether the dog's emotional state is positive or negative rather than indicating the dog's level of excitement.

To see how tail position and pattern of movement combine, let's interpret some of the more common types of tail wagging.

- *A slight tail wag, each swing small,* is usually seen during greetings and can be interpreted as a tentative "Hello there" or a hopeful "I'm here."

- *A broad tail wag* is a friendly "I'm not challenging or threatening you." In many contexts it may also mean, "I'm pleased," and it is the closest thing to the popular conception of the "happiness" tail wag, especially if the tail seems to drag the dog's hips with it.

- *A slow tail wag with tail at "half mast"* is less social than most of the other tail signals. Generally speaking, slow tail wags with the tail in neither a particularly dominant (high) nor a submissive (low) position are signs of insecurity or of being unsure about what to do next.

- *Tiny, high-speed tail movements that give the impression of vibrating* are a sign that the dog is about to do something (run or fight usually). If the tail is held high and vibrating, it signals what is most likely an active threat.

Why Are Some Dogs' Tails Docked?

I F YOU'RE IN the mood to start a heated debate in a group of dog fanciers or veterinarians, just raise the issue of tail docking in dogs. The arguments against this practice are usually based on suggestions of cruelty and mutilation to the dogs whose tails are being removed. This issue has been catapulted into the political realm, and public pressure has caused several countries to entirely ban tail docking. There are, however, two sides to this issue.

Tails are useful. They give important social signals that are interpreted by other dogs. The height of the tail, whether it bristles out or not, the degree of movement or wagging, and even the shape (straight versus slightly cricked or bent) are important communication signs that tell others about the dog's emotional state and social status in the current situation. Some reports have suggested that dogs with docked tails seem more likely to be involved in aggressive encounters with other dogs. The argument is made that these confrontations may result from the ambiguity of the signals sent by the dog with the docked tail.

If tail docking can disrupt canine communication, then why is it done? Many opponents of tail docking claim that it is solely a cosmetic practice, but it did not begin simply as a matter of fash-

ion, with breeders striving for a particular look in the show ring. Many breeds of spaniels that have their tails routinely docked have elegant and well-plumed tails that make the dog appear quite handsome. Historically, however, tail docking began for very practical reasons having to do with the working life of the dog, not its looks.

The first reason for docking tails has to do with guarding. Suppose, for example, that you're a criminal trying to get past a Doberman Pinscher. A long tail would impair the dog's guarding ability because you could simply seize the dog by the tail and thus control its actions while avoiding its teeth. If you could immobilize the dog long enough in this way, an accomplice could severely harm the dog without any threat of injury to either of you. So, in a guard dog a tail might be a liability. For this reason, the tails of many guard dogs are often closely docked. If there's no tail, there's no easy way for bad guys to grab the dog.

Certainly not all of the dogs whose tails are docked are guard dogs. Partial or full tail docking is routine in over fifty breeds of dogs. In many of these breeds, tail docking was originally intended as a simple procedure to avoid a common class of injuries. Tail damage is particularly common in hunting breeds that have to pursue game through heavy vegetation and thick brambles, or over rocky terrain. The natural action of the tail as it whips back and forth can easily lead to a torn, broken, and bleeding tail, which is painful, is often difficult to treat, and may require the riskier amputation of the tail in the adult dog. Obviously, docking the tail early in the dog's life eliminates the risk of this injury.

The usefulness of tail docking was recently proven in a study of German Shorthaired Pointers conducted by the Swedish Council of Docked Breeds. After Sweden banned tail docking in 1989, there was a noticeable increase in the number of tail injuries reported for this breed. In 1991, researchers looked at 191 of these pointers that had undocked tails. The dogs surveyed were, at the time of the study, between twenty-four and thirty months old. An amazing 51 percent of these dogs had sustained tail injuries requiring some form of medical treatment. The likelihood and severity of these injuries appears to be linked to some fairly obvious factors. The scientists mentioned the liveliness of the dog and its tail motions as one factor. How often the dog was used to hunt and the type of terrain traversed were also important factors. Dogs used in bushy, woody, or rocky terrain were much more likely to suffer tail injuries than were those used in marshy areas or on level grassy areas.

Dogs with thicker, well-muscled tails, like Labrador Retrievers, do not have their tails docked and seem less likely to suffer injuries. In some breeds, such as Vizslas, the lower part of the tail is quite strong, but the section of the tail nearer the tip is often turned upward (making it more likely to snag on obstacles) and carries little fat and muscle as protection from brush and rocks. For this reason, only the upper third of the tail is usually docked in this breed. Obviously, then, the tail docking of these dogs as puppies was meant as a means of preventing the kinds of damage that might prove painful and life threatening to these dogs as adults.

Perhaps the strangest reason for docking tails is found with the Old English Sheepdog. Farmers tried to create a breed in which many puppies would be born with virtually no tail at all. When not naturally born without a tail, the puppies had their tails docked from the first joint, down to a length never to exceed two inches. As a result, these dogs were given the nickname "English Bobtails." Why? Well, in Britain in the early 1800s, a livestock tax was imposed. Farmers were taxed for every animal they owned. For the purposes of taxation, "animals" were defined as "all beasts born with a tail longer than a man's thumb." Since many Old English Sheepdogs are born without tails, and the others were docked so young that the tax collectors couldn't tell whether nature or a surgeon was responsible for the dog's current condition, the tax was simply waived for this breed!

Why Do Dogs Howl?

THE SOUND THAT we associate with wild canines, like wolves and coyotes, is the howl. Domestic dogs bark a lot more than their wild cousins but howl a lot less. For wolves the howl has several functions. One of them is to assemble the pack for hunting. Since wolves hunt early in the evening and early in the morning, it is not surprising that those are the times when we're most likely to hear wolves howling. The howls assemble the group, which may have dispersed into the underbrush to sleep through the evening or to rest out of sight during the day. Because our domestic dogs have a food supply that is presented to them by their masters, they do not have to howl to call together their pack so that they can have a synchronized hunt each day.

Howls also serve the social purpose of helping to strengthen the animal's identity as belonging to a pack. When wolves (or dogs) hear the sound of howling, group members gather together and join in singing with their pack. Because howls are a request for social contact, dogs often howl when they are forcibly shut away on their own, or otherwise isolated from their family and pack. This howl of loneliness has the same function as the group howl. It is an attempt to attract other dogs or the people that the dog considers to be members of its pack.

It is important to understand, however, that not all howls are the same. The two most common types are the "yip-howl" and the "social howl":

- The *yip-howl* sounds something like "yip-yip-yip-howl," with the final howl quite prolonged. It usually means "I'm lonely," "I feel abandoned," or "Is there anybody there?" It's the howl that you will most likely get from a dog who has been removed from the company of his family, such as being locked away in a basement or garage for the night.

- The *social howl* is the classic howl, which starts without any fanfare and produces a continuous, prolonged sound. It may occasionally begin with a slightly higher pitch before moving to the main tone, and sometimes the pitch may lower a bit toward the end of the howl. It has a more sonorous sound to the human ear than does the yip-howl, and it is often described as "mournful." This vocalization says, "I'm here!" or "This is my territory!" A confident animal will often howl simply to announce its presence. The social howl is frequently given in response to a yip-howl from another dog, and under those circumstances it means, "I hear you out there!"

Because howls are social sounds, other canines may join the chorus. Once the howling begins, it often turns into a joyous chorus. This vocal performance may go on for quite a while and involve animals from all over a region or a neighborhood. It is during such a wild concert that canines show their musical sensitivity. Recordings of wolves have shown that a howling wolf will change its tone when others join the chorus. No wolf seems to want to end up on the same note as any other in the choir.

What's the Difference between Howling and Baying?

BAYING IS THE sound that hounds make when they're tracking and believe they have found the trail they're looking for. When you first hear baying, it might sound a bit like howling; however, research shows that it is a more complex sound. Baying contains many tone variations, and rather than a single tone being held for a long duration as in a howl, it occurs in short bursts. To me, baying sounds something like the combination of a howl and a yodel. It is certainly a much more excited sound than howling, and it is often filled with a happy enthusiasm.

Hounds bay to indicate that they have the scent of their quarry. In this context baying has some of the same "gather around me" intention that howling does, but the cause is not loneliness; rather, it is seeking cooperation on the hunt. Since at any one time only a few dogs in the pack may have the scent, the baying sound is interpreted by the other members of the pack as meaning, "Follow me! I've got the scent." As the scent becomes stronger, suggesting that the pack is now very close to its prey, the baying becomes a bit less melodious, as the individual sound phrases become shorter in duration but more frequent, and the message now shifts to mean, "Let's get him!" or "All together now!"

The baying sound that hounds make when they're tracking is

extremely important not only to the other dogs in the pack, but also to the humans that accompany them. For hunters, its primary function is to let them know exactly where the pack is at any moment. For both hunters and those who use the dogs in search and tracking tasks, the number of dogs sounding off and the intensity of the baying provide an indication of how strong and fresh the scent is and hence some notion of how near the quarry is. Scientists have demonstrated that it is possible to create Bloodhounds that do not bay, but people who work with these dogs think that that's a bad idea, since it denies them valuable information about how the hunt or search is going.

The sound of a pack baying can be quite melodious, and in the past hunters sometimes deliberately selected hounds to produce the most harmonious combinations of tones. For example, in 1615 Gervase Markham described in his book *Country Contentments* how one could "tune" different packs of hounds for different sounds. For a pack with a sweet cry, Markham recommended including "some large dogs that have deep solemn mouths . . . which must as it were bear the bass in the consort, then a double number of roaring, and loud ringing mouths, which must bear the counter-tenor, then some hollow plain sweet mouths, which must bear the mean or middle part." Finally, he suggested that "amongst these you cast in a couple or two of small singing beagles, which as small trebles may warble amongst them" to provide a balanced symphony.

Does a Howling Dog Mean
That Someone Is About to Die?

THE BELIEF THAT dogs have supernatural or psychic abilities has a long history and is found in many cultures. One of the almost universal beliefs is the conviction that the howling of a dog is a death omen. I encountered an example of this when I was training with the US Army in Kentucky. An old woman whom I knew only as Aunt Lila told me that if a dog gives two howls close together, it signifies that death is coming for a man. Three howls mean a woman. "Dogs look in the direction of the person about to die," she said. "My daddy said it was good luck to have a dog howl with his back to you."

Some people trace the link between dogs howling and death back to Egypt. There the god that took care of the dead was Anubis, and he was represented as having the head of a dog. Thus, a howling dog was believed to be calling a soul to Anubis.

In Ireland the belief is that dogs howl because they hear the noise of the hounds that lead the riders of the wild hunt as they race through the sky and collect the souls of the dying.

The ancient Norse legends have a more amusing explanation, involving the goddess Freya, who was the bearer of love, fertility, and magic, but also the goddess of death. She rode the crest of a storm on her chariot pulled by giant cats. Because cats are dogs' natural ene-

mies, it is said that dogs would start to howl when they sensed the approach of Freya and her mystical felines.

If we ignore any supernatural explanation, there is a simple alternate possibility to explain the belief that a dog's howl is a sign of a coming death. It begins with a well-known thinking predisposition that human beings have. It is a kind of selective memory based on what psychologists call the "confirmation bias," which we encountered earlier when we talked about why people believe that dogs have ESP. Confirmation bias is the tendency for people to notice or even look for events that confirm their beliefs, and to ignore or perhaps undervalue the relevance of observations that contradict their beliefs. In the classic example, someone who believes that a full moon triggers an increase in crime or accident rates will take special notice when such events are reported during a full moon, and will be less likely to notice or remember these same events if they occur at other times. Obviously, over time such a bias would produce an unjustifiable belief in the relationship between a full moon and the occurrence of crimes or accidents.

Now let's turn to the howling dog. Suppose someone in a house is ill. Because of the need to care for that person, a dog who normally stays inside the home might be viewed in this case as a distraction, a bother, or a source of noise that might disturb the patient. For this reason the dog might be put outside, or shut away for a while. Thus, a dog who is normally surrounded by his family, and might even usually sleep in the same room with the sick person, now finds himself alone. We know that dogs howl out of a sense of being alone, and they are trying to call their packmates for social support. The people in the house may be surprised by the dog's unexpected behavior and only remember something like this: "Grandfather's dog never howled before, but the night that he died the dog howled so mournfully because he knew the end was near." The truth of the matter might be that the dog never howled before because he was never locked up and isolated from his family before.

Now we have the setup for developing a superstition. Here are the elements involved:

1. It is common to remove a dog from the house when someone is seriously ill.
2. A seriously ill person may die.
3. A lonely, isolated dog is more likely to howl.
4. We already have a tradition of believing that a dog's howl might be a warning that something bad is about to happen.

Combine such chance associations with our tendency to remember only the cases in which our predictions are correct, and we have all the elements needed to produce yet another example of the psychic ability of dogs to sense the supernatural and predict the future—such as howling when death is near.

Do Dogs Really Use Urine to Communicate Information?

THE DOMINANT SENSE for dogs is the sense of smell. Thus, for dogs, reading scents is much like reading a written message. However, if a dog wanted to write a message to other dogs, what would he use? In many ways, the canine equivalent of ink is urine. Many of the chemicals that give information about a dog's age, sex, emotional state, sexual availability, and health are found dissolved in its urine. Chemicals that produce scents capable of conveying social information are called "pheromones." Dogs even have a special scent detection system called "Jacobson's organ" or the "vomeronasal organ." It is a sort of pancake-shaped pouch of special receptive cells located just above the roof of the mouth, with ducts that open to both the mouth and the nose to allow scent molecules to enter. The large number of nerves and rich blood supply to this organ tell us that it is important to the dog, and this importance is further verified by the fact that there is a special region in the olfactory bulbs of the dog's brain dedicated to processing the information from this special smell receptor.

Because of the pheromones dissolved in it, a dog's urine contains a great deal of information about that dog. Since they are frequent targets of urinating dogs, fire hydrants and trees along a route pop-

ular with other dogs can be a great source for keeping abreast of current events by sniffing. Each tree is really a large dog tabloid containing the latest news in the dog world. While it may not contain installments of classic canine literature, it certainly will have a gossip column and the personals section of the classified ads.

When my dogs are busily sniffing at a favorite post or tree on a city street frequented by other dogs, I sometimes fantasize that I can hear them reading the news out loud. Perhaps this morning's edition goes, "Gigi, a young female Miniature Poodle has just arrived in this neighborhood and is looking for companionship—neutered males need not apply." Or "Rosco, a strong middle-aged German Shepherd Dog, is announcing that he is top dog now, and is marking this whole city as his territory. He says that anybody who wishes to challenge this claim had better make sure his medical insurance is current and paid up."

The biggest difference between dog and human reading is that humans are allowed to finish the entire piece. Many dogs only get to "read the headlines" before they are hauled away by the pull of their leash. This occurs because many owners feel that the process of sniffing where other dogs have left their urine marks is unclean and disgusting. Some unenlightened dog owners may even discipline their dogs for trying to keep up on the neighborhood news.

Why Do Some Male Dogs
Lift Their Legs to Urinate?

THE REASON FIRE hydrants and trees are popular places for dogs to post their urine-scrawled messages is that male dogs prefer to "mark" vertical surfaces. Having the scent above the ground allows the air to carry it much farther. Since dogs often use urine to mark their territory, it is important that the message persist for a while, and a vertical, elevated surface helps the message stay intact longer because rain is less likely to wash it away there compared to horizontal surfaces that collect puddles.

Another extremely important reason for using elevated and vertical surfaces as the target for urine is that the height of the marking tells the neighborhood something about the size of the dog making the mark. Among canines, size is an important factor in determining dominance. Since dominance seems to be more important to males, they have developed the habit of lifting a leg when they urinate so that they can aim their urine higher. In addition, the higher the marking is, the more difficult it is for other dogs to mark over it and obscure the message.

Some dogs engage in the canine equivalent of "image management" using urine as the medium. To convince other dogs that they're the "Big Dog" in their area, they try to get their urine marks as high as possible on the vertical surface that they're marking. Occasionally, you may see dogs almost fall over as they attempt to achieve a higher marking by not only lifting their leg but leaning back to have the stream of urine follow a higher arc.

I once saw a rather bizarre example of an attempt to produce extremely high urine marks. The dog was a Basenji, the small African sight hound that is considered to still be very close to African wild dogs in many of its behaviors. This particular Basenji, a strong, unneutered male named Zeb, had adopted a pattern of urination that is sometimes used by wild dogs. He would aim himself toward a tree and then run directly at it. Zeb would leap when he was near the base of the tree so that his hind feet were essentially walking up the tree. His momentum typically carried him 5 or 6 feet up the trunk. Finally, he would flip over at the top of his run so that he landed on his feet, having performed a perfect loop. The real purpose of this trick was shown by the fact that Zeb performed his acrobatic somersault with a continuous stream of urine flowing from him. Of

course, the ritual left a stripe of urine scent that rose well above those deposited by any other dogs in the vicinity. I often wondered what Zeb's canine neighbors thought as they read his announcement. "Hmm, I think we may have a King Kong–sized dog living nearby," or something like that.

Usually it's males who lift their legs, but it's not unusual for females to do so also. It seems to depend somewhat on the female's self-esteem and confidence. Generally speaking, dominant females are much more likely to lift their legs when urinating, while those who are timid and not very self-assured are less likely to do so. Sexual status also plays a role. Spayed females are much less likely to lift their legs, although dominant females sometimes do even if they're no longer fertile. Environment also plays a role. If there are a lot of sexually active females around, any given female is more likely to lift her leg when urinating. In Denmark, for example, where many female dogs living in the city are not spayed, you're more likely to see the females lifting their legs than you would in the United States or Canada, where most female city dogs are spayed.

Why Do Dogs Like to Sniff Crotches?

HUMANS ARE OFTEN embarrassed when a dog trots over and starts sniffing at their groin, or pokes its nose in their butt. I've already mentioned that the dog's nose is tuned to a set of smells that have a special biological significance to animals—specifically phero-mones, which are scent-producing chemicals secreted by animals to transmit information to other animals. Special sweat glands called "apocrine glands" secrete the pheromones that carry information about an animal's age, sex, health, and even emotional state. In dogs and most other mammals, the apocrine sweat glands are spread over the entire body, with higher concentrations in the genital and anal areas. The pheromone-releasing apocrine cells are even in the hair follicles, so a dog's fur gets coated with these chemicals and becomes concentrated for easier identification by other dogs. Bacteria begin to act on these secretions almost immediately, modifying and inten-sifying the smell. Pheromone smells not only identify the sex, age, health, and mood of the individual, but also carry a lot of sexual information as well, such as where the female is in the estrus cycle, or whether she's pregnant or having a false pregnancy.

In humans the apocrine glands are found only in certain areas of the body, with the highest concentrations in the armpits and groin area, so dogs try to sniff these areas for the same reasons that they sniff the genitals of dogs. As in meetings with other dogs, strangers receive the most attention of this sort, especially if there is a tinge of sexual scent. People who have recently had sexual intercourse seem to attract this kind of attention from dogs. Women who are menstruating or who have given birth recently (especially if they're still nursing their child) will also often find dogs impolitely sniffing at their genital region.

Female ovulation also seems to cause a change in pheromones that attracts dogs. Some researchers noticed that the frequency of crotch sniffing went up dramatically around ovulation and decided to put this fact to use. They trained some Australian Shepherds to pick out cows that had just ovulated, allowing farmers and ranchers to successfully breed these cows during their short fertile period. The dog's "sniff test" is considerably easier and more reliable than most other methods of predicting ovulation. Perhaps this could open up a new class of assistance dogs for humans. Millions of

women, who, for religious or cultural reasons use only the rhythm method of birth control, could be alerted by having specially trained dogs inform them when they are fertile. All this would give a new meaning to the familiar complaint of many husbands that their sex life "has gone to the dogs!"

Even though crotch sniffing is just a natural canine behavior, many people have strong negative reactions when a dog starts examining their body for scent messages. One instance in which this negative reaction to crotch sniffing reached an extreme was the case of Barbara Monsky, a local political activist living in Waterbury, Connecticut. Monsky's reaction was so negative when she was sniffed by a dog that she brought a suit against both the dog, a Golden Retriever named Kodak, and its owner, Judge Howard Moraghan. Specifically, she charged Moraghan with sexual harassment. Judge Moraghan often brought his dog to Danbury Superior Court, and according to Monsky, it was in the courthouse that the dog sexually harassed her when he "nuzzled, snooped, or sniffed" beneath her skirt at least three times. Monsky based her charges on the contention that the judge was complicit in this harassment because he had done nothing about it. Fortunately for dog owners everywhere, when the case was finally brought before US District Judge Gerard Goettel, he dismissed it. In a later interview he explained that "impoliteness on the part of a dog does not constitute sexual harassment on the part of the owner."

Why Does My Neutered Dog
Mount Other Dogs?

MOUNTING BEHAVIOR (COLLOQUIALLY referred to as "humping"), in which a dog clasps the hips of another dog and stands on two legs while thrusting his own hips, is part of sexual behavior in dogs. In most common canine interactions, however, it has nothing to do with sex, but a lot to do with social dominance.

You can see that mounting behavior can be relatively independent of sexual intentions by watching the behavior of very young puppies. Well before they've reached puberty (which comes at about six to eight months of age), they already show this kind of activity. Mounting in puppies appears shortly after they begin walking and when they start playing with each other. It is a socially significant behavior, not a sexual one. For young puppies, mounting is one of the earliest opportunities for learning about their physical abilities and their social potential. It basically represents an expression of dominance. The stronger, more authoritative puppy will mount its more submissive brothers and sisters simply to display leadership and dominance. These behaviors will then carry on into adulthood, with the significance being power and control, not sex.

Because mounting behavior is used as a signal for dominance and can be unrelated to reproduction, its social significance applies

to both males and females. As a display that serves to challenge or to assert social dominance by one dog over another, this behavior can occur between individuals of the same or the opposite sex. A male mounting another male is thus not displaying homosexual tendencies, but is simply saying, "I'm boss around here." Females may use mounting as a statement of social position as well. Females can be dominant over other females and even over male dogs, and can display this dominance by assuming a mounting position.

This is not an issue of sexual confusion, since the dynamic structure of dog society is not a question of gender alone. Status in the canine world depends more on size and physical ability, combined with certain characteristics associated with temperament, motivation, and drive. The traditional interpretation is that in the social structure of dogs there are three different hierarchies:

- The overall rank in the pack starts with the leader at the top and moves down to the ultimate underdog.

- There is a lead, or alpha, dog for each gender—that is, an alpha male and an alpha female—and one of these will be the overall pack leader.

- The males and females below the alpha dogs each have their own additional ranking.

Mounting behavior may be used to assert dominance in any one of these rank orders, so you may see males on males, females on females, males on females, or females on males. None of these behaviors represent any form of sexual advance or invitation. Instead they should be viewed as a very clear signal of serious social ambitions by the mounting dog. The dominant or "top" dog is literally the dog that is on top.

Because mounting behavior is most commonly an attempt to claim a higher social status in relationship to another animal, it should not be surprising that the belief that you can stop a dog from mounting by neutering him is just a myth. Neutering will eliminate certain sex-related hormones in the dog, such as testosterone, and the reduction in these male hormones will tone down a male dog's aggressive tendencies and reduce some of the dog's other dominance behaviors. In this way, it may reduce the appearance of mounting behaviors. However, neutering will not change the dog's basic character and personality, which means that a neutered but dominant, leadership-oriented dog may still engage in mounting behavior. What removal of the sex hormones will do is reduce the intensity with which the dog pursues its social ambitions. However, the older a dog is at the time of neutering, the less his dominance traits will be curtailed, since exposure to testosterone will have already shaped the development of his brain.

Though mounting behavior is something that not many people

find acceptable in their dog, in comparison to dogs actually fighting, with a full display of gnashing teeth and slashing attacks, it is really quite controlled and harmless.

Often dogs attempt to mount humans. Given that mounting behavior is most typically a statement of dominance, it should now be clear that a dog who has grabbed your knee and is merrily thrusting away is not saying "I love you," nor is it simply trying to be "amorous." When dogs mount human beings, they are virtually always attempting to express their feelings that they're dominant. In effect, they want to be leader of the pack. This kind of "talk" from a dog is not permissible. It should be stopped to maintain the normal social hierarchy, which should always put humans above canines in dominance.

Why Do Dogs Roll in Garbage, Manure, and Other Smelly Stuff?

I HAVE OFTEN HAD people ask me why their otherwise apparently sane dog will roll around in garbage or dung or something equally offensive to the noses of humans. One man even told me that he stopped walking his dog along the shoreline because whenever a dead fish or a mass of seaweed containing rotting organic matter washed up on shore, his dog would make a beeline for that smelly mess and immediately begin to roll in it. The dog would usually walk away with a stench that required it to be bathed or at least hosed down before it could be allowed in the house afterward.

Several theories have been proposed to explain why dogs like to coat themselves with distasteful, strong odors. One of the silliest of these theories is that the behavior is a means of fighting parasites. The notion is that insects, such as lice and fleas, wouldn't hang around on something that smelled so bad. Unfortunately, most insects do not seem the least bit put off by bad odors on a dog, and in fact, many insects are attracted to such smells because they usually signify the presence of decomposing organic matter, which is a great source of nutrients for insects.

A second theory claims that rolling in smelly stuff is a means of writing a message to other members of the pack. Dogs and wolves seem to like rolling around in things that smell bad, but if you pay attention you'll see that what they choose to anoint themselves with is always organic, such as dung, rotting carrion, and so forth. Since the wild ancestors of dogs were not only hunters but also scavengers, much of the stuff that they're rolling in could still possibly be edible. The notion, then, is that the wild canine rolls in this material and then returns to the pack. The other members of the dog's group immediately pick up this scent and know that there's something that can pass for food nearby. If such were the case, however, one would expect that when a wild canine arrived back at the pack with its new odor, the pack members would immediately start backtracking toward the site where their packmate came from. This is certainly not the usual case.

A third theory suggests that the dog is not trying to pick up odors from the stinking mess it rolls in, but is actually trying to cover that smell with its own scent. It is certainly true that dogs and wolves often roll around on something, like a stick, a new dog bed,

or such, as if trying to deposit their scent on it. Some psychologists have suggested that often the reason a dog rubs against a person is to leave a trace of its scent and to mark the individual as a member of the pack, much the way that cats rub up against people to mark them with their odors.

The explanation that makes the best evolutionary and adaptive sense is that this stinky behavior might be an attempt at disguising the dog. The suggestion is that we're looking at a behavior left over from when our domestic dogs were still wild and had to hunt for a living. If an antelope smelled the scent of a wild dog or jackal or wolf nearby, it would be likely to bolt and run for safety. For this reason, wild canines learned to roll in antelope dung or carrion. Antelopes are quite used to the smell of their own droppings, and carrion is common on the open plains where many animals live. Therefore, antelope and other prey animals are less likely to be frightened or suspicious of a hairy thing that is coated with that smell than they are to be afraid of the same visitor smelling like a wolf. Disguising itself with misleading odors allows the wild hunting canine to get much closer to its prey.

Perhaps the most speculative theory begins by noting that for human beings, our dominant sense is vision, while for dogs it is the sense of smell. Like people, dogs enjoy sensory stimulation and may well be prone to seeking such stimulation to an excessive degree. Therefore, it could be argued that the real reason canines roll in obnoxious-smelling organic manner is simply an expression of the same sense of aesthetics that causes human beings to wear overly loud and colorful Hawaiian shirts.

Why Do Dogs Touch Noses?

S OME CANINE BEHAVIORS are extremely common, but we seldom think about them, and when we do we often have no idea
(or the wrong idea) as to why they occur. A simple example is the fact
that dogs meeting other dogs often begin their social exchange by
touching noses. For those of us who have studied animal communication, this snout contact appears to be part of a greeting ritual. It
is actually more common in cats than in dogs, where the nose touch
may sometimes be accompanied by rubbing against the body of the
other animal or continued sniffing of the other's head or body. Cats
use this greeting nose touch with virtually any cat they meet that
appears nonthreatening.

Dogs appear to be more selective than cats in their nose-to-nose
touching. Not every greeting is accompanied by snout contact. However, it is quite common for adult dogs to engage in nose touching
with puppies. It is also quite common for dogs to use nose touching
when greeting another nonthreatening species. Thus, dogs can be
seen touching noses with cats and kittens, horses, and so forth. A
young human child crawling across the floor is often greeted with a
nose touch by an approaching dog.

Some casual research that I've done suggests that nose touching

can be an important part of the socialization of puppies. For a number of dog breeds known to sometimes be nippy as adults (such as
Corgis) I've suggested that while the dog is still a puppy, the people
in the family and any friends or acquaintances that can be enlisted
to help should engage in nose touching with the pup. Doing this
seems to speed socialization and reduce the likelihood of nipping
incidents later in life. In all breeds, this early nose touching with
humans appears to make the approach of people, or their looking
directly into the dog's eyes, less of threat as the dogs mature.

While most canine researchers recognize the ritual greeting
aspect of nose touching in dogs, recent research published in the
journal *Animal Behavior* suggests that there may be another, more
pragmatic reason for nose touching. Marianne Heberlein and Den-
nis Turner at the University of Zurich's Institute of Zoology set up
a situation in which a dog could explore a room while another dog
observed the first dog's behavior. Let's call the dog who is watch-

ing the "observer," and the dog who is exploring the "actor." Here's how the experiment works: First, the actor has to know that there's a treat hidden in the room. So the actor is allowed to watch while a couple of dog treats are placed in one of four positions around the room. Next, screens are placed in front of each position, again while the actor is looking. At this time the observer dog is brought into the room. The observer watches while the actor is let loose. As you might imagine, the actor will run behind any screen where he saw the treat hidden.

Up to now things are straightforward. The observer dog doesn't know why the actor dog ran behind the screen, because it can't see the treats. Sometimes, however, the experimenters secretly remove the treats while putting the screens in place. Therefore, sometimes the actor dog finds the treats and gets to eat them, while other times he runs behind the screen only to find that there are no treats.

Finally, the two dogs are allowed to interact. As might be expected, they often touch noses as part of the greeting ritual. What's surprising is that if the dogs touch noses and the actor dog has just come back from successfully finding and eating a treat, it is much more likely that the observer dog will quickly run to investigate the area behind the screen where he saw the actor go. If the actor dog has not found and consumed some treats, it is less likely that the observer dog will go to that place to investigate.

The researchers therefore conclude that nose touching between dogs not only is a way of saying "Hello" but also helps answer the question "Have you encountered any snacks or other food around here?" The answer is to be found on the breath of the other dog, and where the food may be found comes from where the observer dog has seen the actor go before

These findings confirm what everybody who knows dogs suspects. Dogs are naturally sociable and friendly, but much more so when they think food might be involved.

How Well Do Dogs Understand Human Body Language and Communication Signals?

M OST DOG OWNERS have had the experience of simply glancing at where their dog's leash is hanging, only to find that the dog is now headed for the door anticipating a walk. While this seems like an everyday event to dog owners, it has special significance to scientists because of what it indicates about how dogs think. First of all, it shows that dogs have the ability to read human body language and intentions. In addition, it shows that dogs understand that our movements and gestures may contain important clues as to what will happen next in their world.

For decades, scientists have been studying "social cognition" in dogs. The term refers simply to how well dogs read cues in the behavior of others. As humans, we do this automatically. For instance, we know that when the person we're talking to starts glancing at his or her watch, we had best get to the point quickly. All social mammals have evolved remarkably discriminating ways of reading the signals sent to them by their group members—normally members of the same species. However, recent research shows that dogs are surprisingly good at reading certain types of social cues in humans.

The experimental setup used to test for such perception in animals is quite simple. Start with two inverted bucket-like containers.

Place a morsel of food under one of them while the dog to be tested is out of sight. Of course, you must make sure that both containers have been rubbed with the food so that there is no scent difference. Now, give some sort of signal to indicate which bucket actually contains the food. The most obvious signal would be to tap the bucket containing the food. Less obvious would be to point your finger at it. An even more subtle signal would be to tilt your head or body toward it without pointing. The most understated signal of all would be not to move your head or body but simply to look with your eyes toward the correct container. If the dog chooses the right container, he gets the food. All this may sound simple, but for most animals it's not.

Daniel J. Povinelli, a psychologist at the University of Southwestern Louisiana, found that, surprisingly, our closest animal relatives, chimpanzees, initially perform quite poorly at this task. (Actually, so do three-year-old human children, although they are better than the apes.) However, both chimps and kids can quickly learn to read the correct cues. The real surprise came when a team led by Robert Hare of Harvard University ran the same test on dogs. The dogs could immediately interpret the signals indicating the location of the food four times better than the apes could, and more than twice as well as the young children, even if the experimenter was a stranger.

So the real question is, where did dogs get this talent? The first guess might be that since dogs are descended from pack-hunting wolves, the ability to pick up social signals evolved to help coordinate the hunt. If so, one would expect wolves to be at least as good at the bucket task as dogs. However, testing shows that wolves are worse than chimpanzees and a lot worse than dogs at reading these signals.

The next guess might be that dogs learn to read human language because they hang out with and watch their human families. This theory would suggest that young puppies, especially those still living with their littermates and not yet adopted into human families, would be poorer at picking up human signals. However, this is not so; even nine-week-old puppies, still living with their mother and littermates, do better than the wolves and chimps. This means that this ability was not inherited from the last common dog-wolf ancestor, and it does not require tremendous exposure to humans to develop.

So where do dogs get their superior ability to read human signals? Scientists have now turned to a consideration of evolutionary changes that occurred during dogs' domestication. Obviously, dogs that could figure out their masters' intentions and desires would have been more likely to thrive in a human-dominated environment and hence produce more young. But were specific dogs initially chosen to be domesticated *because* they had a better ability to understand people? Or was the improved ability some sort of unintended by-product that arose during the process of domestication? Unfortunately, the scientific jury is still out. We simply don't have enough data to decide whether humans deliberately chose dogs that could better understand our social signals, or whether this ability is a "hitchhiker" trait that came along on the evolutionary ride to domestication. Regardless, this ability is yet more proof that our domestic dog is definitely not merely an urban-dwelling wolf that has learned to sport a veneer of civilization in order to get free room and board. Rather, it supports the notion that the dog is a separate species that evolved, or more precisely *coevolved*, with humans and may well understand the emotions and intentions of humans better than any other species does.

PART 4

How Do Dogs Learn?

Compared to Other Animals, How Smart Are Dogs?

JUST HOW INTELLIGENT are dogs when we look at their mental abilities relative to other animals, or even in comparison to other mammals? Comparing the intelligence of animals of different species is difficult, although certain tests and problem sets have proven to be useful. However, making the tests equivalent for, say, a dolphin that lives in the water and a horse that lives on land is complicated and may prove to be virtually impossible. Charles Darwin claimed, "Intelligence is based on how efficient a species became at doing the things they need to survive," but one might argue that by that definition, all species that stay healthy, remain numerous, and avoid extinction are equally intelligent.

Such problems have prompted psychologists and biologists to look for a technique to assess intelligence that doesn't require specific tests or even the cooperation of the animals involved. It starts with the argument that a bigger brain must be better, since it allows more memory storage and faster processing because it has more neurons and neural connections. For example, a person with a brain size of 1,500 cubic centimeters would have an average six hundred million more cortical neurons than a person with a brain size of

1,400 cubic centimeters. So the first guess might be that animals that have bigger brains must be smarter.

Initially we see that humans have larger brains (averaging 1,400 grams, about 3 pounds) than dogs (averaging 72 grams, about 2½ ounces for a 20-pound Beagle), with the rhesus monkey falling in between (at 97 grams, about 3½ ounces), and all this makes sense in terms of our general impression of the relative intelligence of these species. Looking at brain weight alone, however, we would be forced to conclude that the elephant with its 6,000-gram (13-pound) brain is brighter than a human, and that the supergeniuses of the Earth are whales; for instance, the sperm whale has a brain that averages 7,800 grams (about 17 pounds). The problem is that larger animals have larger brains. They need to in order to control the movements of their larger masses of muscles. They also need a larger brain to process sensory information; for example, every added square centimeter of skin surface will need more cortical neurons to process the senses of touch, heat, cold, and pain from that region of the body.

In the late 1970s, the psychologist Harry J. Jerison developed an alternative measure that he called the "encephalization quotient," or EQ. The EQ is a mathematically sophisticated comparison of the actual brain weight of an animal compared to the expected brain mass for that animal's body size. This measure compensates for the fact that bigger animals tend to have bigger brains and shifts the question to one of whether the animal has a larger or smaller brain than what we would expect for an animal with its body mass.

Species	EQ
Man	7.44
Dolphin	5.31
Chimpanzee	2.49
Rhesus Monkey	2.09
Elephant	1.87
DOG	**1.76**
Cat	1.00
Horse	0.86
Sheep	0.81
Mouse	0.50
Rat	0.40
Rabbit	0.40

According to the encephalization quotient, the brightest animals on the planet are humans, followed by porpoises, great apes, and elephants. The dog is close behind elephants in its EQ. Descending down the list, we find cats and then horses, sheep, mice, rats, and rabbits. As a general rule, animals that hunt for a living (such as canines) are smarter than strict vegetarians (you don't need much intelligence to outsmart a leaf of lettuce). Animals that live in social groups are also smarter than solitary animals, because they must engage in reasoning like, "If I do this, then he'll do that, so I can do the other thing." This means that the social chimpanzee is smarter than the solitary orangutan. The fact that dogs are much more social animals than cats probably explains why dogs show up as being smarter than cats as well.

Are Some Dog Breeds
More Intelligent Than Others?

J UST AS EVERYONE wants to have smart kids, most people
want to own clever dogs. However, whether a dog is "smart" or
"dumb" depends on which aspects of its behavior we consider. For
example, was Nobel Prize–winning physicist Albert Einstein intelligent? Obviously, to derive the theory of relativity required a mathematical genius. Yet Einstein was so bad at simple arithmetic that
his checkbook was always out of balance.

Intelligence has a variety of different dimensions. In human
beings we might subdivide intelligence into verbal ability, numerical
ability, logical reasoning, memory, and so forth. The intelligence of
dogs also has several different aspects, among which we recognize
three major dimensions: *instinctive intelligence*, *adaptive intelligence*,
and *working and obedience intelligence*.

"Instinctive intelligence" is what a dog was bred for. For example, herding dogs were bred to herd animals. Their ability to round
up animals, keep them close together, and drive them in a particular
direction is inborn and requires human intervention only for keeping it under control and giving it a bit of direction. Different breeds
obviously have different types of instinctive intelligence. Guard
dogs watch over things, retrievers fetch, hounds track or pursue,

pointers sniff out birds and indicate their location by pointing, and companion dogs are attuned to human social signals and respond to our moods to provide comfort. Every dog has an instinctive intelligence, but it is senseless to make comparisons across breeds as to which are "smarter" in this respect; their abilities are simply too different to compare.

"Adaptive intelligence" is a measure of what a dog can learn to do for himself. It includes learning and benefiting from experience with the environment, solving new problems, and so forth. Adaptive intelligence can differ among individuals of the same breed. For example, although all Golden Retrievers have the same instinctive intelligence and most are quite clever, you will occasionally encounter one that seems totally clueless and makes the same mistakes over and over. The difference between the various Goldens is a matter of difference in adaptive intelligence, and this can be measured with appropriate tests.

When most people think of dog intelligence, they might think of dogs working their way through complex obedience exercises in an obedience ring or on a stage. They might also think of highly trained animals such as police dogs, guide dogs for the blind, hearing assistance dogs, or search-and-rescue dogs. A dog responding appropriately to its master's commands and signals tends to give us the impression that we're viewing the peak of dog intelligence. Thus, when dogs demonstrate through their responses that they understand particular commands from a human, they are demonstrating one of the most important aspects of their intelligence. This aspect is important because if dogs did not respond to human instruction, they would not be capable of performing the utilitarian tasks that we originally valued them for, and therefore they would never have been domesticated and wouldn't be with us now. This third type of intelligence in dogs is appropriately called "working and obedience intelligence." It is the closest to what we might call school-learning ability, and it is based on what the dog can learn to do when instructed by humans.

It should be possible to rank dog breeds in terms of their working and obedience intelligence. Using statistics from kennel club records based on obedience competition trial results doesn't work because these results get mixed up with popularity. For example, in one recent year, according to American Kennel Club (AKC) trial records, Otterhounds earned no obedience degrees, while Golden Retrievers earned 1,284. This result doesn't tell us that Otterhounds are stupid, however; there were approximately 670,000 Golden Retrievers registered with the AKC, while in that same year there were only 300 Otterhounds. Even if Otterhounds were the most brilliant of all dogs, and if every registered Otterhound earned an obedience degree in the test year, that would amount to only 300 obedience degrees compared to the 1,284 degrees for Golden Retrievers.

While their records can't help us assess dog intelligence, the kennel clubs do provide us with another resource—namely, the dog obedience judges themselves. These individuals are trained to observe and evaluate how dogs perform under controlled conditions. It is not unusual for a judge to spend twelve to twenty hours on any given weekend judging and scoring dogs of various breeds. In addition, most judges are also dog trainers, spending many more hours observing and working with dogs. Because of this extensive experience watching and evaluating dogs, if any one group of people should have the accumulated knowledge of the relative performances of various breeds, it is dog obedience judges. They see each dog perform under the same conditions, and they should be able to separate the quality of the performance from the number of competitors.

For my book *The Intelligence of Dogs* (Free Press, 2006), I contacted all of the dog obedience judges registered with the AKC and the Canadian Kennel Club, and provided them with a long questionnaire that allowed them to rank the various breeds in their working and obedience abilities. Despite the length of the questionnaire, 199 judges (approximately half of all the obedience judges listed in North America) provided complete information.

The degree of agreement among the judges was amazingly high, suggesting that real observable differences were being reliably detected. For example, when we consider the dogs ranked highest in obedience or working intelligence, we find that 190 of the 199 judges ranked the Border Collie in the top ten. There was somewhat less agreement as to which breeds showed the poorest working or obedience intelligence, yet even here the degree of agreement was still high among my sample of experts. Of the 199 judges, 121 ranked the Afghan Hound in the bottom ten.

According to the judges' rankings, the top ten dogs in terms of working and obedience intelligence are, in order:

- Border Collie
- Poodle

- German Shepherd Dog
- Golden Retriever
- Doberman Pinscher
- Shetland Sheepdog
- Labrador Retriever
- Papillon
- Rottweiler
- Australian Cattle Dog

while the bottom ten dog breeds (moving downward) are:

- Basset Hound
- Mastiff
- Beagle
- Pekingese
- Bloodhound
- Borzoi
- Chow Chow
- Bulldog
- Basenji
- Afghan Hound

Does this mean that everyone should rush out and get one of the top ten breeds of dogs? Definitely not! While a smart dog will learn everything you want it to know, it will also learn everything it can get away with. In the end you may have to spend much more time "civilizing" your clever dog to learn the limits of acceptable behavior in your household.

Does this mean that we should stop breeding the dogs low in the rankings to "improve the species"? Definitely not! Every dog has an instinctive intelligence for which it was bred. The Afghan Hound, at the bottom of the working and obedience list, was bred to spot, pursue, and pull down antelope and gazelle. If you ever saw one of these dogs running, you would appreciate how refined that skill is. In addition, most dogs in our urban society were chosen as companions. Did you take the time to give an intelligence test to the last *person* you were considering as a possible spouse, lover, or companion?

Finally, some of the dogs lower in the intelligence list have other laudable qualities. The Afghan Hound is arguably among the most beautiful of dogs. I notice that every year *People* magazine has a special issue presenting "The 50 Most Beautiful People in the World." I don't remember *People* ever having an issue featuring "The 50 Most Intelligent People in the World." Just think about what we consider to be the most important aspects of humans; well, the same applies to dogs!

Which Works Better—Reward Training or Discipline-Based Training?

W HEN YOU DECIDE you want to modify the behavior of your dog (or another human being), there is one fundamental decision you must make—namely, whether you will base your training methods on rewards or punishments or some combination of the two. So-called discipline-based training programs tend to use punishment as a major tool, taking away privileges, inflicting pain, or effecting some other negative outcome if the individual fails to behave in the desired manner. That's the way governments work, fining you or jailing you if you do not behave as they want you to. For dogs, the punishment may be in the form of a leash jerk, shock from an electronic collar, scolding, slapping, or the like. The alternative is reward-based training, in which each desired behavior results in a good outcome, such as a treat or praise, and wrong behavior simply does not result in a reward.

Obviously, we want to use the most effective form of training, so the question is, Which works better and produces the best outcome: reward-based training (so-called positive training) or discipline- and punishment-based training? There are several answers to this question, but let's look at just one of the most important ones.

When we're talking about learning, we are actually talking about

some form of relatively permanent change in behavior that comes about because of an individual's experiences in the world. More than two hundred years ago the philosopher John Locke described learning as forming an association, which is a mental connection between events that occur in a particular sequence. Most people understand this as learning a relationship between an action and an outcome, such as learning that clicking a wall switch turns on the room light, while sticking your finger in an electrical outlet produces a painful shock.

There is however a form of learning which the average person either does not know about, or seldom thinks about, called "classical conditioning." However it is a very important and fundamental form of learning through which associations are formed between events occurring in the real world and reflexes or emotional responses in the individual. The word "conditioning" is just psychological jargon for learning, and "classical" is applied because it was the first form of learning to be that was scientifically studied.

Classical conditioning was first systematically studied by Ivan Petrovich Pavlov, a Russian physiologist. Pavlov's research on this topic started with a casual observation. He was studying the salivary secretions in dogs and knew that when he put food in an animal's mouth, it would always salivate. He also observed that when he worked with the same dog on several occasions, the dog would begin to salivate when it observed things associated with food, such as the food dish or even the sight of the person who normally brought the food. Pavlov recognized that the dog's response showed a unique form of learning because it involved a response that can't be controlled voluntarily. For example, if I said to you, "Make your mouth water," you would find it virtually impossible to set up a constant flow of saliva simply by willing it. Pavlov realized that something special was occurring in the canine responses he observed: an involuntary action (salivation) that is usually triggered only by a certain class of events (food) was now being controlled by a new stimulus (the sight of the experimenter).

Pavlov studied this process using a simple procedure. During training he presented a neutral stimulus (one that doesn't ordinarily cause a dog to salivate), such as the sound of a bell, immediately before he puffed a bit a meat powder into the dog's mouth to trigger salivation. A few repetitions of the ring-puff-slobber sequence would then be followed by a test with just the sound of the bell. Sure enough, the bell, which originally had no effect on the dog, would now cause it to salivate. The nature of the neutral stimulus made no difference; it could be a click, a light, a drawing, a touch, or anything else. The important thing was that now the dog was responding to this previously neutral stimulus as if it were the meat powder—by salivating. The dog doesn't have to want this to happen or participate actively in the learning process; it will just happen on its own.

Why should we care about training our dogs to drool on cue, when many of us are already bothered by the amount of drooling

they do naturally? The truth of the matter is that we're not interested in drooling; the real importance of classical conditioning is
that it is the way in which we learn to attach emotional responses to
things. All we need is a sequence in which we encounter a stimulus
followed by an event that triggers an emotion. After just a few repetitions of the stimulus-event-emotion sequence, the stimulus itself
will trigger the emotion, because of classical conditioning.

The most famous example of how classical conditioning can produce learned emotional responses was provided by John Watson,
who conducted an experiment that would never make it past the
ethical review panel in any of today's research institutions. Watson
showed a rat to an eleven-month-old baby named Albert. Albert
demonstrated no fear of the rat at all. Next, Watson showed Albert
the rat and, at the same time, had someone bang two metal rods
together to cause a loud clanging sound. The sound startled Albert,
frightened him, and caused him to cry. After a few repetitions of
this sequence—rat-clang-fearful cry—just the sight of the white
rat would cause Albert to cry and try to crawl away. He not only acted
afraid of the rat, but now Albert seemed to be afraid of any furry
object, including white rabbits, stuffed toys, fur coats, and even a
Santa Claus beard. Watson concluded that he had classically conditioned the emotion of fear and attached this emotion to white furry
objects in Albert's mind. Notice that Albert did not have to want
to learn or actively participate in trying to learn this fearfulness; it
happened automatically, simply because the stimuli were associated
with something that triggered his emotional response.

Classical conditioning of emotions provides one example of
evidence suggesting that reward-based training procedures should
work better and establish a stronger bond between dog and trainer
than punishment-based systems can. Every time you give the dog a
treat or some other reward, you set up the following event sequence:
sight of you–treat–pleasant feeling. Even if your timing is off and

you're not a very good and knowledgeable trainer, no harm is being done in attempts at reward-based training. Every instance of reward makes it more likely that the dog will feel better about you, because you're actually conditioning the emotional response of a pleasant feeling following the sight of you.

The flip side of this coin is the use of punishment or harsh corrections. The sight of you or your hand or the training leash and collar, immediately followed by pain or discomfort, will ultimately come to be associated with negative feelings and avoidance.

You can often see this effect for yourself if you visit various dog training establishments and dog obedience schools. In those that tend to use discipline and punishment, the sight of the trainer and his training equipment will often cause the dogs to run to the back of their kennel and act as if trying to avoid the entire situation. They appear to find their trainer unpleasant to be around. Such a relationship will certainly have a negative impact on the dog's training. In contrast, the approach of the dog trainer who uses reward is apt to cause the dogs to rush forward cheerfully with their tails wagging. They obviously have formed a positive emotional bond with this trainer and are eager and happy to continue their education.

What Is Clicker Training?

I N RECENT YEARS a lot of attention has been given to something
called "clicker training," which is viewed by some people as a more
efficient way of training your dog. Before I describe clicker training,
however, it is important to understand that even though the basic
principle behind dog training is really quite simple, successful appli-
cation of this principle may not be easy. By analogy, think about
playing a piano. The basic principle is simple: all you have to do is to
press the keys corresponding to the notes you want to hear. However, years of practice may be required before you can do it right.

The basic principle behind teaching your dog any new task is that
*any behavior that is rewarded will be strengthened and the likelihood that
it will appear will increase, while any behavior that is not rewarded will
be weakened and the likelihood that it will appear will decrease.* That's
it! To train a dog, it is not necessary to understand the underlying
neurological or chemical events, or to know which brain centers and
pathways are involved. Often the "tricky" part, however, is getting
the animal to perform the behavior in the first place so that we can
reward it. It is also necessary to get that reward to the dog at the
right time, so that the appropriate behaviors will be strengthened.
This process may require a fair bit of time and effort.

Suppose I'm trying to teach my dog to come on command. What I need to do is reward the dog when he's moving toward me after I give the command "come." However, if I rush out to give the dog a bit of kibble as a reward, he will stop moving toward me in order to get the treat into his mouth. Notice that this means that the reward has actually interfered with, or stopped, the behavior I wanted the dog to perform. What I was looking for was a sequence of events in which the dog was rewarded while coming toward me, which would strengthen that approach behavior, but what I really did was reward the dog for ceasing to move in my direction. Because the basic principle of dog training is that the behavior that occurred immediately before the reward is what is strengthened, if I continued doing the same thing I would actually be teaching the dog to take a few steps toward me and then stop. What we need, then, is a reward that doesn't stop the behavior—a reward that can be precisely delivered while the behavior we want is occurring and that we can deliver from a distance.

Clicker training is based on creating a special reward of this nature. It uses the classical conditioning of emotions that we mentioned in the previous section. Here, the idea is to select a signal that makes the dog feel good but does not interfere with his ongoing behavior.

To create this new reward, you first have to decide what kind of signal you want to use. In recent years the sound made by a hand-held clicker has become popular, but the signal can actually be anything—a whistle, a light, a word, or any specific action. I prefer using my voice, since that leaves both of my hands free for other things, and I use the word "yes" said in an enthusiastic tone. I know a dog trainer, though, who uses the word "click" as a signal.

Once the signal is chosen, you have to "charge it" with positive emotional value using classical conditioning. The easiest way to do this is to use food rewards. Suppose we've chosen the click of a mechanical clicker as the signal. To turn this sound into a reward, all we need to do is repeat the sequence of a click followed by a rewarding treat a number of times. After we repeat click-treat, click-treat, click-treat enough times, the clicking sound will take on many of the positive properties of the actual food reward. We have now created a learned, or "secondary," reward. It may help you understand this concept if you recognize that most of the rewards used to control human behaviors are secondary rewards. Basic or primary rewards are biological, such as food and drink and sex. Secondary or conditioned rewards include money, grades in schools, praise, promotions, medals, awards, and titles, and so forth. The rewarding qualities of all of these have been learned through association with primary rewards, although the chain may reach back into the distant past. For example, the rewarding value of praise may trace its origins back to being fed by your mother, who accompanied the placing of food in your mouth with words like, "That's a good boy" or "What a pretty girl." The importance of creating a signal, such as

a click, that has positive emotional qualities is that it can be used to reward the dog without interfering with the dog's behavior, and later, when convenient, it can be followed by an actual food reward to keep it emotionally "charged."

What should be clear is that clicker training is not actually a teaching method, but rather a technique for creating a special reward that can be used to assist us when we're training a dog using the four basic methods of dog training, which are *behavior capture, lure training, physical prompting,* and *shaping.* Next we'll examine each of these methods in some detail.

What Is Behavior Capture?

PROBABLY THE SIMPLEST form of dog training is "behavior capture," which is sometimes called "autotraining" because the dog seems to be automatically training himself. In theory this technique is extremely simple. All you have to do is to wait until the dog spontaneously performs the behavior that you want to train, and then you label it and reward it.

As an example, suppose you have a puppy with the highly original name of Rover that you want to train. All you have to do is watch Rover's activities carefully when you're interacting with him. As the puppy begins to move toward you, label the activity by saying "Rover, come!" and then quickly follow that with a reward, perhaps a treat or a pat. In the same way, when the pup begins to sit, you say "Rover, sit!" and give him a reward. For this training technique to work, the dog must be rewarded at the end of each action—just as if he had performed the behavior because of your command. Each reward strengthens the association between the command words that you use as a label, and the dog's actions. After a few repetitions the command should become connected with the behavior and the reward in the dog's mind. When this happens, the dog should begin to give you the behavior after you say the words.

There are several potential problems with behavior capture. One obvious problem is that it might take a while before the dog actually performs the behavior you want to train, but simple behaviors, like sitting, lying down, coming to you, and so forth, occur frequently enough to be easily "captured" and trained in this way. Once the dog understands that there's a reward waiting if he engages in a particular behavior, he will usually treat the experience as a pleasant game. It may take him a few "guesses," though, to figure out which behaviors produce the reward and which don't. During the process the dog will make many mistakes, but this is normal. Mistakes are actually helpful, since in the same way that actions that are rewarded develop stronger associations, unrewarded actions grow weaker. Think of it this way: the more mistakes your dog makes, the sooner he learns what is *not* going to be rewarded. In the end the dog will eliminate the unprofitable options and start repeating the actions that earn him what he wants.

Dogs seem to enjoy this process, and it is simple enough that you can even get young children to join in the training. Behavior capture is an especially helpful technique when you're dealing with fearful, shy, poorly socialized, or aggressive dogs, since it seems to focus their attention and calm them down.

You can probably already see another potential problem with this method of training—namely, getting the reward to the dog instantaneously, without interrupting the action. This is the same problem we looked at when we talked about clicker training. The point is we want to reward the dog while he's doing the behavior that we're trying to teach him. Rushing out at full speed because the dog is coming toward you in response to your command to come so that you can give him a piece of kibble as a reward is apt to stop his movement toward you. Your sudden movements may even cause him to believe that he has done something wrong. The result might be that the dog stops, in which case you're rewarding him for stopping—

not coming—or you might even frighten him and cause him to dash away from you and to later act uncertainly or unhappily when he hears the word "come." It is here that a learned reward—whether a click from a clicker, the words "good dog" or "yes," or whatever other signal you've chosen as a reward—comes into play.

Once you've created your secondary reward using the procedures described in the previous section on clicker training, behavior capture becomes really easy. Now as the dog begins to move toward us, we say, "Rover, come!" and immediately follow the command with the learned reward, which might be a click, the words "good dog," or whatever. When the dog finally reaches us, we can then give him a primary reward (a food treat), to help strengthen the association and to keep the learned reward "charged" with positive emotions. When a learned signal is used in this way, some animal trainers call it a "bridging stimulus" because it bridges the time gap from the instant that the dog performs the correct action to the moment when we can actually give him a treat.

Behavior capture is especially useful when you want to teach the dog activities that are difficult or impossible to enforce. For example, when you're housebreaking your dog, you can wait until the dog begins to squat or raise a leg to eliminate and then label the action. You could use labels like "be quick" or "hurry up" and repeat the label once or twice during the elimination process, following each phrase with the learned reward, such as "good dog." When the entire action is finished, you reward the dog with a treat. It should only take a few weeks until using the command, "Rover, be quick!" begins to cause the dog to sniff around and choose a place to eliminate. In this way, some aspects of the dog's elimination can be placed under direct control.

For fun, you can teach your dog some simple tricks using behavior capture. For example, if your dog spontaneously sits up on his hind legs in anticipation of a treat, you can simply label the action with something like "beg for it" and then give him a reward. After a few repetitions, the dog will treat the label "beg for it" as a command and respond by sitting up. You have "captured" his casual behavior and turned it into a trick.

What Is Lure Training?

ONE PROBLEM WITH behavior capture as a training method is that you have to wait around until your dog performs the action that you want to teach him. "Lure training" is a more effective hands-off method of training, since you actually induce your dog to perform the actions that you want using a lure. The most effective and most commonly used lures are bits of food in the form of kibble or other treats.

A simple test to see whether your dog is ready to proceed is to move a food lure up and down in front of the dog's nose. If the dog follows the lure with his eyes and head, causing him to nod in agreement, he is ready for training. If you can move the dog's head, then you can move the dog's whole body, so you can use lure training to teach body positions (such as sit, down, and stand), or control the direction of the dog's movements (come, roll over, spin, go right, go left), and even get him to focus his attention on specific objects or people that you want the dog to attend to.

If your dog does not follow the kibble with his nose, begin by using something more enticing, such as a favorite toy, but it really helps if you take the time to teach your dog to work for kibble. I teach every dog I have to like food before I start to train it. Puppies can easily be taught to appreciate food, simply by hand-feeding individual pieces of kibble throughout the day, rather than all at once from a bowl at mealtimes. Do not waste valuable training lures and rewards by feeding your dog from a bowl. Soon your dog will enjoy the kibble from your hand even more than playtime.

Here's how lure training works. Suppose you want Lassie to sit on command. If you can lure her to move her nose, the rest of her body will follow. First show the dog a treat, and then slowly lift the food lure upward and backward. The path you're following with the lure moves directly over your dog's nose and then back between the eyes toward the back of the head. As Lassie looks up to follow the movement of the food, her rear end will naturally lower into a sitting position. If she jumps up, then you're holding the food lure too high. Next, just as in behavior capture training, you say, "Lassie, sit!" followed immediately by your learned-reward sound

("yes," "good dog," or a click) followed by a treat. Finally, release your dog with a happy "OK!" or "All done!" and a quick pat (this will automatically come to be the release command for any behavior). With the sit command, it is important that you give the treat and learned reward before the dog gets up, so in the early stages of training you will have to be fast. Repeating this sequence a few times, sometimes when the dog is at your side and sometimes when she's in front of you, will quickly give you a reliable sit command. Keep in mind that you have not really taught your dog how to sit, since she knew how to sit when she was only a puppy. What you've done is to teach Lassie to sit *on request*. The essence of training is that we don't care much about when the dog decides to sit on its own accord; rather we want her to sit when we ask her to.

Once the dog will sit reliably, say, "Lassie, down!" and lower a piece of kibble just in front of her nose, moving it forward and downward toward the floor directly in front of her. As the dog lowers her head to follow the food, she will usually lie down. Don't worry if your dog stands instead; just keep the kibble hidden under the palm of your hand until she lies down. As soon as she does, say, "Good dog!" and give her the food.

As the dog learns to watch the movement of your handheld lure, your hand movements soon become effective hand signals. Hold your hand palm-upward for the "sit" signal, and palm-downward for the "down" signal. After a few repetitions, your dog will begin to anticipate each hand lure signal on hearing your verbal command. After a number of repetitions, the verbal request will replace the lure, since it successfully prompts the desired response. At this point food lures are no longer necessary to entice your dog into each position, because a hand signal or verbal request is sufficient.

Once your dog is performing reliably, you can begin to fade out the lure. Put the treats in your pocket and now mimic the luring movements with your hand but with no food visible, while still giving the verbal command. When your dog does what you want, she still gets the learned reward ("good dog," click, etc.) followed by the food treat from your pocket. Next, begin gradually making your movements smaller, and soon the dog will be responding to the verbal command alone. When the dog is performing well, you should start to phase out the food—sometimes giving the dog only the learned words of praise, other times giving both praise and food. Gradually wind down the number of food rewards, only randomly giving the dog a treat for performing, but never decrease the learned rewards. Those words of praise should be there virtually every time the dog does what you ask her, since they evoke the same good feelings that an actual food reward does.

Lure training is really quite simple; even children can effectively train a dog using it. Dogs seem to like it, because they treat it as a game in which they can win treats by figuring out what their trainer wants from them.

Both behavior capture and lure training have the advantage of training your dog without any assistance from the leash. The lack of a leash gives the dog the idea that he can benefit from obeying your commands even when not physically connected to you by the lead, and even when you're some distance away. This mind-set in the dog is very helpful and gives you much more reliable control over your pet.

What Is Physical Prompting?

THE EARLIEST SYSTEMATIC methods of dog training that have been recorded depended heavily on leashes, collars, and "physical prompting." In those early days the term "prompting" might be too mild a description of what was actually happening. The idea was that a dog was given a command and then physically forced into the position desired. Thus, the early training manuals described a method of teaching your dog to sit on command that involved issuing the command "sit" and accompanying it with a tug upward on the leash with one hand, and pushing the dog's rear end down with the other hand, thereby forcing the dog into a sitting position. To get the dog to lie down, you tugged downward on the leash, sometimes grabbing the dog's collar to assist you, or sometimes grasping the dog's legs to force them forward while you press on his shoulders to enforce the down position. Getting a dog to heel (that is, to walk on a loose leash by your left side) involved a series of pops and tugs to keep him from forging ahead or lagging behind and to ensure that he was by your side.

The first dog training manuals were written for use in training service dogs by the German military. They were consistent with the theory that was used in training soldiers—namely, that individuals must perform whatever actions were requested, and if necessary they were forced to react as desired or punished for not doing so. Later, as psychologists began to learn more about the process of learning, it was argued that physical prompting was an easy way to get the dog to do what you want especially if you followed the prompted behavior with a reward. It was argued that this method was psychologically rational, since the learning principle is that the last behavior the dog performed before it was rewarded is what will be strengthened, and prompting simply involves forcing the dog to do what we want so that we can reward it. The truth is that physical prompting is really quite complicated and takes an experienced trainer to do well. Good timing, expert leash handling, and absolute consistency are needed, and most people need a lot of practice before they can master it.

If dog training using physical prompting is done properly—and that means with good timing, and in a *gentle*, *patient*, and *nonthreatening* manner—this method can work. A side benefit is that, when done well, physical prompting involves direct handling of the dog, and with the trainer's hands all over her pet as part of the training, the bond between the owner and the dog will strengthen. Unfortunately, especially when used by novice trainers, physical prompting is seldom done well.

To begin with, some dogs simply resist being placed into positions, and what was supposed to be a physical prompt turns into a wrestling match between the handler and the dog. Giving the dog a treat once he has actually achieved the desired position in this case may not be rewarding the act of sitting or lying down, but rather rewarding the act of the dog's bracing or resisting our efforts while we're trying to get him into that position. In other words, we may really be rewarding the dog for trying *not* to sit or lie down.

I've already spoken about how emotional responses can be learned. So if we look at the method of physical prompting, it is

important to be honest and recognize that a sharp jerk on the leash is unpleasant. Thus, if we use leash tugs as prompts, we are associating unpleasant emotional responses with the sight of the leash and collar, and perhaps also to the general setting associated with training. If we combine an unpleasant leash jerk upward with a hard push down on the dog's rear, we may be teaching a negative emotional response to our hand touch as well.

Finally, since the dog must be restrained by the leash throughout training, we are not promoting good off-leash control but rather telling the dog that he needs to respond to commands only when you're physically connected to him because that is the only time that you can actually enforce your will and that is the only time that he gets any rewards.

For all of these reasons, dog training based on physical prompting as the primary method of teaching has become less popular, although some traditional dog trainers still rely on it.

What Is Shaping?

A LTHOUGH THE METHODS of dog training that we've discussed so far can work well, they have some limitations. Some behaviors are unlikely to occur spontaneously, which means that they can't be trained by behavior capture. Some behaviors are too complex, or have too many steps, to lure or physically prompt the dog. To teach these kinds of behaviors, we use a technique called "shaping" or sometimes "successive approximations." Shaping is based on the idea of rewarding behaviors, or parts of behaviors, that gradually become closer and closer approximations to the actions that we really want to teach.

Back in the 1950s, the well-known Harvard University psychologist B. F. Skinner, who is credited with doing the research that led to our basic understanding of how shaping works, demonstrated this method of teaching using, as an example, how to train a dog to ring a bell that was hanging across the room on a wall. Skinner pointed out that the first thing you have to establish is exactly what your target behavior will be. In this case, the desired behavior is simply to push against the bell to make it ring. Next you must split the behavior into as many simple parts as is practical. Each of these simple behaviors will be trained by behavior capture and will be rewarded with a learned reward signal (here we'll stick with the word "yes") followed by a bit of food. So in this case the list of the dog's behaviors might look something like this:

1. He turns his head and looks in the general direction of the bell.
2. He turns his whole body in the direction of the bell.
3. He takes a step in the direction of the bell.
4. He takes several steps in the direction of the bell.
5. He moves one-quarter of the way to the bell.
6. He moves halfway to the bell.
7. He moves three-quarters of the distance to the bell.
8. He moves all the way to stand near the bell.
9. He goes to the bell and looks at it.
10. He brings his nose near the bell.

11. He touches the bell with his nose.
12. He pushes hard enough against the bell with his nose to make it move.
13. He pushes hard enough against the bell to make it give a sound.

Notice that we're progressing in very small steps, and each step must be mastered before we go to the next one. The point in using small steps is that we want to make it more likely that the dog will give us the next behavior in the sequence so that we can capture it and reward it. Once we have that behavior, we can proceed to the next level. So for the first step, for example, it is likely that at some time the dog will spontaneously turn its head away from us and look in the general direction of the bell, at which point we can quickly say "yes" and follow it with a treat. The dog rapidly learns that treats are available during training, if he does the right thing. In essence, we're setting up a situation in which we're asking the dog to think for himself. If we have done this correctly and we could read the dog's mind, the dog going through a shaping procedure might be saying to itself, "How do I get that treat? What do I need to do? Let's try this. That didn't work. Let's try a something else," and so forth. The more behaviors the dog is willing to try, the more likely it is that he will give us the behavior we want, which we can then capture and reward.

The learned reward (the click or word of praise) has to be given as soon as the dog makes the response that you want and before he moves on to something else. The real difference between good and great trainers is how precisely they time that learned reward. Good trainers must also be good observers; otherwise they might miss behaviors that should have been rewarded. The training also has to be a fairly flexible process. If the dog seems to be having difficulty with one step, then the trainer must go back a step or two to try to keep the momentum going. If the dog is still having difficulty with one step, the trainer should see whether the step can be divided into simpler parts that the dog can master. Each step must also be trained reliably enough that it can serve as a platform on which the next step can be built. However, once the dog has learned a step, the trainer must move on to the next step and fade out the reward for the previous one.

At first this kind of training usually moves fairly quickly, but it may slow down as the requirements become more complex. The trainer must be alert, in order to find ways to give the dog enough rewards to keep him from getting frustrated or quitting. If any signs of anxiety appear, the trainer has to go back to a step that the dog has already perfected and then start moving forward from there again.

There is still some dispute about when you should introduce the actual command for the behavior. For simple behaviors like sitting or lying down, which don't have to be shaped, the command ("sit" or "down") is usually given just as the dog is starting to perform the correct behavior. When trainers are teaching a shaped response sequence, they often wait until the dog is reliably performing the action before starting to add the command. So in the case we've been dealing with, if the dog is dashing toward the bell and we know that he's going to ring it, we might add "Lassie, ring it." I personally like to use a nonverbal command right at the beginning, such an arm motion to prompt the dog to start moving, and then, when the dog is actually doing what I want him to do, I add the spoken command.

Most dogs learn to look forward to the times when you're training them using the shaping procedure. Once the dog knows that this is a training session, he'll usually start to show you all the behaviors he already knows, just to quickly figure out which ones you'll be rewarding this time. Clever dogs learn that if you don't reward the behaviors they already know, they should be trying something different, so they'll often offer behaviors that you haven't seen before just on the off chance that this is the one you want to reinforce this time. This side effect of training a dog by using successive approximations makes it easier to capture new behaviors that may be useful in the future.

What Are the Limits of Canine Learning?

I T IS DIFFICULT to know exactly how much a dog can learn, and recent data keeps pushing the limits beyond what we felt was possible before. Perhaps one breakthrough, in terms of our ability to assess the intelligence of dogs, came about in the early 1990s. At that time it dawned on me that one way to learn about the limits of canine abilities was to use tests that had been developed for assessing human infants, and to modify them so that they could be used for dogs. The idea was that if a dog can pass a particular test, he, like a human child being tested, has clearly demonstrated he has the mental ability that was being evaluated. However, the added advantage was that, using the outcome of the test it might be possible to assign a human mental age equivalent to the dog's performance. Comparing the dog's performance to that of a human child in this way might give us a clearer idea of the dog's mental capacity. Apparently I was correct, since a number of canine behavioral researchers ultimately adopted the same strategy.

My own first research using this technique began when I was looking at canine language-learning ability, as described in my book *The Intelligence of Dogs*. I began by modifying the MacArthur Communicative Development Inventory, which contained several forms to assess language and communication ability in very young children, not only in terms of the use of words, but also in terms of gestures. Using only family pets that were not specifically trained to understand language and gestures, I came to the conclusion that, on average, dogs had the mental ability roughly equivalent to that of a human two-year-old. Further work led me to believe that the most intelligent dogs might have mental abilities similar to those of a two-and-a-half-year-old human child. I cautioned that we really didn't know how far we could push the dog's abilities until we specifically tried to train a dog for maximum comprehension of human language.

If my estimates were correct, then it should be possible to train a bright dog to understand two hundred words or more. Several years after my initial research, scientific reports appeared con-

firming that a Border Collie named Rico, who had been specifically trained to improve his vocabulary, had a language ability in that range. Since that time, a number of researchers have tried to see just how much language a dog can learn. At the time of this writing, perhaps the most linguistically advanced dog is a Border Collie named Chaser, who is owned by a retired psychologist named John Pilley. Chaser's vocabulary is around a thousand words—the equivalent of what we might expect from a human three-year-old. Chaser understands not only single words, but also concepts and categories like "ball," which may include a number of items of different sizes and textures. Chaser's skills did not come easily, however; they required a lot of training, with Dr. Pilley often spending four or more hours a day working with the dog. It therefore seems likely that Pilley's research is pushing the limits of what a dog can be trained to understand.

The idea that a dog's learning ability might hover around that of a two- or three-year-old child has to be understood within a certain set of limits. Dogs are more athletic and physically accomplished than are human children of that age, and therefore they can learn jumping and swimming feats that children cannot be expected to accomplish, even though such children would understand the concepts of jumping or swimming. On the other hand, children have better manipulative abilities than dogs, thanks to our fingers and opposing thumbs. In addition, some tasks depend on sensory ability, so asking dogs to learn things that depend on fine color discrimination, or asking children to learn tasks based on scent discrimination, would obviously be inappropriate.

Finally, it is important to limit our conclusions to mental and intellectual abilities, since in terms of social consciousness, with their interest in sex, dominance, and ranking in a social group, dogs are more like human teenagers in their intellectual functioning.

If we are to draw a conclusion from this kind of research, it is that dogs have a mental ability approximating that of humans between two and three years of age, at least as far as language, object recognition, and concept formation go. This means that a problem or task that would be too difficult for a human two- or three-year-old to solve or learn is likely to be beyond the dog's capacity as well.

PART 5

Is There Something Special about Puppies and Old Dogs?

How Are Puppies Created?

GIVEN THE NUMBER of dogs in the world, it is surprising how little the average person knows about canine pregnancies and births.

A female dog (technically called a "bitch") is fertile and willing to accept a male dog for mating only when she is "in heat" or "in season." The scientific label for this three-week-long phase of the female's life cycle is the "estrus period." The term "estrus" derives from Greek and Latin terms used to describe "frenzied passion," which certainly seems to be descriptive of the female dog's willingness to entertain many partners during this time interval. Generally speaking, most breeds have two estrus periods per year, although the intervals between one period of heat and another may actually vary between six and nine months. Wild canines, like wolves, have only one estrus cycle per year, and some dog breeds that are closer to their wild ancestors, like the Basenji and the Rhodesian Ridgeback, follow that pattern and come into season only once a year.

In human females, vaginal bleeding during menstruation indicates a period of infertility, but in dogs the indication that a female is about to go into heat starts with a bloody discharge that then turns clear (although some dogs may continue to show blood spots throughout the estrus period). Although the bitch remains in heat for about twenty-one days, she generally allows dogs to mate with her for only about ten days, usually starting around day nine. During this time, if you touch the base of the female's tail she will hold it clamped to the side, to allow a male to mount. Some breeders refer to this as "hussy" behavior. The actual period of fertility occurs when the vaginal discharge stops and the eggs are released (ovulation). This is a much narrower window of time, lasting only about four to seven days.

The normal duration of pregnancy in dogs is about fifty-eight to sixty-five days (eight to nine weeks). During the first few weeks there is no visible change in the female. As her hormonal balance begins to change, the first indication that the dog is expecting may be enlarged mammary glands, which make her teats become visible after about six weeks into the pregnancy. At this time after the end of the estrus period, some unspayed females who have not been bred may show signs of a "false pregnancy." Typically, a female experiencing a false pregnancy will gather toys, slippers and other objects; build a nest; and perhaps try to mother the objects she has gathered as if they were puppies. Normally, this behavior disappears on its own.

The canine uterus is shaped like the letter "Y" with one "horn" of the "Y" on either side of the abdomen. If the mating has been successful, then each of these horns contains a series of developing embryos, which fill it like peas in a pod. It is often possible to tell whether the bitch is pregnant by using palpation (gentle pressure of the fingers) and even to count the number of puppies in the litter. This can be done between four and five weeks after conception, but it is not possible much later than that, because the uterus becomes too filled with fluid and thus it becomes impossible to feel the individual "bumps" which will each become a puppy.

The expectant mother signals that the birth of her pups is imminent by apparently losing her appetite about a day before delivery. She will become restless and will seek out some place she has chosen to deliver, and it may not be the lovely new whelping box her owner has prepared for her.

Shortly before labor begins, the female's first water bag will break. There is one for each pup. When it breaks, the water bag leaves a puddle that looks much like urine. The dog's contractions then begin to slowly build, with the first pup delivered within about two hours after the onset of labor. Each subsequent pup will be delivered at intervals of ten to seventy-five minutes, alternating between the left and right horns of the uterus. Small litters often produce larger puppies that have more difficulty passing through the birth canal and thus take longer to be born. Larger litters with smaller pups usually pop out much more quickly.

During the process of creating specific dog breeds, humans have made the birth process more difficult for some. In very small breeds, like the Yorkshire Terrier, a Cesarean section (which involves surgically opening the womb and removing the puppies) may be needed. The same is true for some breeds, like the English Bulldog, that have been bred to have heads that are too large to pass safely out through the mother's vagina.

Generally speaking, the number of pups in a litter varies by breed, with smaller breeds having fewer puppies. At the other end of the spectrum, we might consider Tia. She was a Neapolitan Mastiff, which is a large dog that may stand 29 inches (75 centimeters) at the shoulder and weigh in excess of 150 pounds (70 kilograms). In 2005, this large dog gave birth to a litter of twenty-four puppies!

Why Are the Pups in Some Litters So Dissimilar and Mismatched?

I T IS QUITE striking the way puppies in some litters look so similar to one another that they give the impression of being clones, while other litters contain pups that display a variety of shapes, sizes, colors, and personalities. These varied outcomes are all a matter of genetics.

The general principle is that the more similar the parents are in appearance, size, and behavior, the more similar the puppies will be. Thus it should not be surprising that litters of purebred dogs will tend to be much more uniform than mixed-breed litters. The reason is that pure breeds have been manipulated through selective breeding so that there is much less genetic variability from dog to dog and within a breed. Certain characteristics have been "fixed" so that they are predictable characteristics of the breed, including body shape, color, and basic behavioral predispositions. For example, in a litter of Golden Retrievers, one should never find a black dog or one with spots or colored patches. The reason we can count on certain characteristics being the same within a breed is what geneticists call "homozygosity," which is just a technical term meaning that dogs of the same breed have similar genetic material. So, if you breed a pair of Cocker Spaniels, you will never find something that looks like a Bulldog in the litter. It is much like having a pot of chicken broth:

every time you dip a ladle into the pot, you will find it full of chicken broth and nothing else, simply because it is such a uniform soup.

However, if you're mating dogs of different breeds, the situation changes drastically. Now you're dealing with what geneticists call "heterozygosity," which is a broad mixture of different genes. To go back to our soup analogy, we're now looking at a vegetable beef soup, made with large chunks of different vegetables. If we dip a ladle into this mixture, one time we may come up with some chunks of beef, some potatoes, and some peas in our broth, while another time we may get little beef and few potatoes but there may be lots of peas, carrots, and onions in the ladle. So with mixed-breed dogs, all bets are off. As an example, suppose you cross a Scottish Terrier and a Poodle. Some of the resulting pups may look like Scotties and others like Poodles. There may also be some strange mixtures, like something that looks like a long-legged Scottie, or a square-faced Poodle, or a curly-coated terrier, and so forth.

In addition to the mixing of breeds, in dogs there is another reason why the pups in a litter may not look or behave alike: some of the dogs in the litter may have different fathers. In purebred dogs produced by conscientious breeders, a lot of care is taken to make sure that this won't happen. However, it can occur because female dogs

produce a number of ova (eggs) at the same time, which is why they have litters of pups rather than one at a time. When the female ovulates, the ova are still immature, and they will continue to mature over the next two to three days after ovulation. Even though they are immature, however, some have progressed far enough to be successfully penetrated by sperm, and after ova have fully matured they will remain available for fertilization for another two to seven days. If we look at the male side of the reproductive act, we find that canine sperm can remain alive and capable of performing their functions for up to eight days. Now add the behavioral components—namely, dogs are polygamous breeders who will mate with anyone available, and females remain receptive to male suitors for a week or more—and the situation can get complicated. This means that if Mommy is a party girl, her pups might look quite different from each other because, although they came from the same litter, they had different daddies.

Why Are Puppies Born with Their Eyes and Ears Closed?

As MAMMALS EVOLVED, each species, in effect, had to make a choice. It had to select strategies for reproduction and development that would give that species and its offspring the best chance to survive in their particular environment. The alternative selected also had to fit with the usual patterns of behavior that the animals engage in to stay alive. Because they give birth to live babies, the choice for mammals is whether to have a long pregnancy and produce fully formed and functional offspring, or to have a short pregnancy and produce immature, partly formed offspring that are helpless and take a lot of care.

At one extreme we have animals like deer and cattle. For example, the gestation period for a cow is nine months. A newborn calf weighs 55–99 pounds (25–45 kilograms), and its brain is fully formed. In terms of sense organs, it can see and hear efficiently. Most importantly, it can run well enough to keep up with the herd. Biologists refer to species that produce relatively mature and mobile offspring as "precocial," from the word "precocious," which refers to the characteristic of exceptionally early development or maturity, as in a precocious child who shows mental maturity beyond what we would expect for the child's age in years. Obviously, for a species whose ability to run away from predators can determine its survival, being born mature is a necessity.

The various canine species, including dogs, represent the other extreme. In the wild, canines survive by hunting. Carrying a litter of puppies slows the female and makes it difficult for her to catch faster-moving prey and to do her part in the coordinated hunting of the pack. Therefore, getting the pups out of the womb and onto the ground quickly is an advantage. In addition, between hunts (which can be spaced days apart), there is not much to do, so the female has time to care for helpless infants. When she's out pursuing food, the pups can be safely stored in a den.

The gestation period in dogs is short, only about two months— fifty-eight to sixty-five days on average; however, the trade-off is that newborn puppies are quite helpless. Biologists refer to species that produce immature, dependent offspring as "altricial"—a word derived from the Latin root meaning "to nurse," "to rear," or "to nourish." It refers to the need for the young of these species to be fed and taken care of for a long period of time.

Many of the puppy's critical organs, including its brain, are not fully formed at birth and will spend several weeks developing rapidly. The same is true of the eyes. So, the reason that puppies are born with their eyelids tightly shut is that the eyes themselves are still developing and are extremely fragile. They need the protection that the closed eyelids provide, serving as a barrier to protect the immature

optical system from potential damage by foreign objects, such as dirt or grit, or even pathogens. In addition, exposure to too bright a light at this time might possibly damage the still delicate photoreceptors and optical mechanisms.

Most puppies begin to open their eyes at about two weeks of age, but even then the eyes are not fully developed and functioning perfectly. It takes several more weeks before their eyes mature and their eyesight begins to approach normal.

In the same way that puppies are born with their eyes closed, they are born effectively deaf because their ear canals are closed. Relative silence is important for the developing ears, since sounds involve changes in pressure that mechanically move structures in the mature ear. Forcing the puppy's fragile auditory machinery to respond to sound inputs before it is fully developed could cause great damage to the basic apparatus needed to hear.

The ear canals begin to open at about the same time the eyes open, but when they do open, the ears are much more fully formed than the eyes are at this point in time. Usually, within a week or so after its ear canals begin to open the puppy's hearing is fully usable and quite acute.

Why Do Puppies' Eyes Start Out Blue?

WHEN PUPPIES FIRST open their eyes at about two weeks of age, their eyes are blue. Typically, this is a grayish blue that may appear "milky," but an icy blue or even an aqua with a hint of green are possible alternatives. While this blue color might appear attractive, it is actually evidence that the pup's eyes are still immature. In this case the immature portion is the iris, which is the colored portion of the eye, that has not yet fully developed. The purpose of the iris is to adjust the amount of light reaching the eye by varying the size of the pupil (the dark hole in its center that allows light into the eye). To effectively block light from everything except the pupil, the iris is pigmented, and that pigment absorbs light. However, that pigment is slow in developing.

You might be thinking, "But isn't blue a pigment?" Actually, in this case the blue color does not come from the eye's pigment, but from a physical principle called "Rayleigh scattering." This is the same principle that makes the sky appear to be uniform blue. It is based on the fact that when light encounters anything that it might be reflected from or bounce off of, the shorter wavelengths (those that appear blue to us) are dispersed and scattered to a greater extent. So in the case of the sky, when sunlight encounters moisture molecules or dust particles, the short blue wavelengths are effectively smeared over the area to give the sky its blue appearance. The same thing happens to light entering the lightly pigmented iris of a puppy, causing the iris to appear blue to us.

The blue color is eventually lost, as pigment begins to fill into the iris over a period that may take up to two months. Ultimately, the eye will take on its mature color, which ranges from virtually black, through browns, to sometimes a pale golden yellow depending on the breed. There are some exceptions—most familiarly, breeds that include the Siberian Husky and some herding dogs, such as Collies, Shetland Sheepdogs, and Australian Shepherds, where, in a number of individuals, the dark pigment level remains low and the eyes always appear blue.

A similar process happens in humans. Although babies of African and Asian descent are usually born with brown eyes that stay brown, Caucasian babies are often born with steel-gray or dark-blue eyes. Over the next nine months the pigment density builds up, and although some eyes may stay gray or blue, many turn green or hazel, while the majority turn brown over time—just like the eyes of most puppies.

Why Do Puppies Sleep in a Pile?

E SPECIALLY DURING THE earliest few weeks after being born, puppies in any litter can usually be found sleeping in a heap, squeezed close together and often on top of one another. There are two reasons for this behavior. The main one has to do with warmth.

Remember, puppies are born in a fairly undeveloped form, and in their first two or three weeks they even lack the ability to maintain their own core body temperature. The normal body temperature of an adult dog is 101°F (38°C), but puppies usually begin life being able to generate an internal heat of only about 97°F (36°C). Their average body temperature will slowly rise over a few weeks to normal, but until that happens they are completely dependent on their environment to provide adequate warmth. This is the reason why, if you visit most good breeders, you will find that they attempt to provide some form of additional heat for the pups. Typically, an electric heating pad may be used, perhaps a small space heater out of the reach of the pups, or perhaps a heat lamp suspended at a safe distance over the puppies' living area. As an alternative, the puppies' living area might be placed next to a radiator or heat register. It is important that the heat level not be too high, since the puppies'

mother has to spend time there as well and overheating can be a problem in adult dogs.

Fortunately, in the puppy's environment another source of heat is close and easily accessed: its littermates, which radiate body heat. Typically, sleeping puppies end up in a pile because, one after another, the members of the litter try to snuggle close together, often crawling on top of or trying to burrow under their brothers and sisters in an attempt to obtain body heat from their littermates.

The second reason for the pile—a reason that becomes more important as the puppies develop further—is that young dogs are extremely sociable and crave the company of other living things. If they are socially isolated from other pups or their mother, they become distressed and distraught. Thus, each pup serves as a social presence for its littermates and obtains social comfort for itself by huddling close enough to the other young pups in the brood so that it can feel their touch. If all the puppies in the group try to crowd together to feel the comforting presence of one another, the result is a pile of puppies.

Why Do Some Puppies Go Limp
When You Pick Them Up?

ONE OF THE oddities of puppy behavior is their response when they're picked up. You look at them bouncing around the floor, playing and tussling with their littermates, running with that exuberant but still slightly uncoordinated energy, and then you pick one up and it is as though you turned off an electric toy. Inexplicably, the puppy goes as limp as an overcooked piece of spaghetti, its muscles slack; and it may even close its eyes.

What you are seeing here is a response that has been carried over through evolution. In the wild, canines, such as wolves and the other ancestors of our domestic dogs, kept their puppies safe by keeping them in their dens, especially if there was potential danger nearby. If you watch a mother dog retrieving her pups, you will see her grab them by the scruff of the neck, and she'll lift and carry them back to the safety of the den. To make it easier to get all the pups to safety quickly, the moment the pup feels the support of the ground fall away, it goes limp. Struggling would only potentially hurt it or raise the anger of its mother. Pups who struggle might even be left behind, while those who do not are quickly brought out of harm's way. Given the way evolution works, more of the pups that submit

and do not struggle will survive, so the behavior becomes fixed in future generations of puppies.

This behavior does not persist forever. Over time, the likelihood that the pup will go limp when lifted diminishes. Once the puppies enter the equivalent of adolescence, like all teenagers they begin to actively resist attempts to control their behavior. Once they reach that phase, picking up the young dog is more like trying to hold a whirling dervish rather than a limp dishcloth.

Why Do Mother Dogs Clean Up after Their Puppies for the First Few Weeks?

NEWBORN PUPPIES ARE so helpless and immature when they're born that they can't even urinate or defecate by themselves. They actually need the help of their mothers to stimulate these very basic actions. The mother dog will lick the urogenital and anal areas of the pups to trigger their peeing and pooping. This service on the part of the mother continues for about three weeks, by which time the pups can see and hear and also have the ability to stand and move around (even if still quite unsteadily). At this point in their development, the pups no longer need their mother's stimulation to initiate toilet behaviors.

During the early helpless period, and for some time afterward, the mother cleans up after its pups. Cleaning involves licking off and swallowing the urine and fecal matter. In so doing, the mother is expressing an important behavior passed down through the evolution of wild canines and other animals that live in dens. In the wild it is important for the den to be inconspicuous. If it smelled of the droppings of those that lived in it, it could be more easily discovered by predators. So the mother cleans up because the instincts associated with the den are still strong, and as soon as possible she will begin to "instruct" the pups to empty themselves outside of the den.

It is this same "clean den instinct" that allows dogs to be housebroken. Once a dog comes to view the entire house that he lives in as his den, he will be strongly inclined to do his business outside, away from the living area. This is also the reason why cattle, horses, and monkeys can't be housebroken, because they have no instincts associated with a clean den.

Although, to human sensibilities, the idea of eating urine and fecal material seems offensive, the material eliminated by puppies is not all that noxious. Since the waste material is simply what remains after the mother's milk is digested, and that substance is a very efficient source of nutrition with little additional indigestible material, puppy urine and stools have very little odor and apparently very little taste (or at least nothing that tastes bad to the mother). It is this same diet of only mother's milk and the action of the enzymes that break it down that seems to give puppies a special sweet-smelling breath that I have heard described as "a misty swirl of milk and honey."

All of this sweetness and innocuousness seems to change once the puppies' diet begins to include more solid food. Apparently, the waste associated with that new diet contains components that make the puppies' droppings much less palatable and will also tend to leave the puppies with the more familiar doggy breath scent that we find in adult dogs. With this change in taste, the mother becomes less inclined to clean up after her brood. These developments have several effects: One is that the mother tends to push the pups out of the den for longer and longer periods of time during the day, making it more likely that they will develop the habit of eliminating at a distance from the place where they normally sleep. The mother will also spend less time in the den herself, meaning that she is not so available for nursing. With less time spent nursing, the mother's milk production begins to slow. All of this is part of the weaning process, which will ultimately cause the pups to begin to forage for themselves and to adopt a more self-sufficient lifestyle.

How Old Is Your Dog?

DOGS GROW MORE quickly than people, and they don't live as long. Many people like to convert the age of their dog into the equivalent in human years, to give themselves some idea of where the dog is in its life history. You may have heard that 1 year in a dog's life is equal to 7 years in a person's life. That's not really true. That estimate came about when the average age that people lived to was supposed to be around 70 years and the average life expectancy of dogs was presumed to be about 10 years. On the basis of life expectancy alone, then, people calculated that each year in a dog's life was equal to 7 years of human age.

The fatal flaw in the system of equating 1 dog year with 7 human years is quite simple. In their first year puppies grow and change very quickly, and their physical and psychological development proceeds much faster than does human development in these early stages. Thus, if our calculation were correct, a one-year-old dog would be physiologically equivalent to a human seven-year-old. However, at one year of age a dog is quite capable of producing puppies, which is why by their first birthday, many pet dogs have already been neutered or spayed. In comparison, how many seven-year-old boys and girls do you know who are able to create a baby? At the other end of the life span, consider a dog that is 12 years old. Twelve years is a pretty long time for a dog, but most dogs who make it there still can get around pretty well, unless they are susceptible to arthritis. If each dog year equaled 7 human years, a dog who lived to age 12 would be 84 years of age in human terms, and except for some senior athletes, there aren't all that many people in their mid-eighties who move as agilely as a midsized 12-year-old dog. So let's redo the calculation in light of current science.

At the age of 1 year, your dog has all the physical abilities that a 16-year-old person has. At 2 years old, your dog is a lot like a 24-year-old human. For the next 3 years (until your dog is 5), each birthday adds approximately 5 human years. However, to go beyond that fifth birthday we have to add another variable.

With all other factors held constant, generally speaking larger dogs tend to have shorter life spans than smaller dogs. This difference becomes important after the dog passes five years of its actual, chronological, age. From that point on, for small dogs you add 4 years of human life for each real year of age, while for medium-sized breeds you add 5 years of age, and for large breeds you add 6. These are round numbers that reflect the way your dog's body is changing in comparison to human developmental changes. While this scheme may sound complicated, it is really quite a simple calculation.

Suppose we want to calculate the human equivalent age for your 12-year-old Miniature Poodle, which, for the sake of argument, we will classify as a smaller dog. We start with 24 years for the dog's first 2 years, and then add 5 years each for the next 3 years. This brings us to 39 years in human age. Now for every additional year in the remaining 7, we add 4 years of age, or a total of 28 years. Adding that to the previous 39 years gives us a human equivalent age of 67, which is a youngish senior dog. If you were dealing with a medium-sized dog, you would add 5 years for each year beyond the first 5, which would add 35 years to the 39 from the first 5 years, for a total of 74 years in human life. Right now, 74 years is the average length of life for people, and 12 years is the average life span for midsized dogs. For the largest breeds, we would be adding 6 years for each of the years past the age of 5, which would make the dog 81 years in human age, which is old by most standards.

While this calculation works fairly well in most instances, the actual rates of aging for a particular dog will also depend on its breed, how well it is cared for, and some additional factors.

Can Old Dogs Develop
Alzheimer's Disease?

N O ONE KNOWS exactly why dogs or humans decline in their abilities when they age. One theory suggests that as the genetic material (DNA) reproduces itself in each new cell, the successive transcriptions become less accurate, sort of like making copies of copies of copies on a photocopier, where each one gets progressively grainier and harder to read. Damage to the DNA can also come about because of natural radiation from cosmic rays and more terrestrial sources (such as breathing in air pollutants or fumes from certain solvents), which in turn might lead to faulty enzyme production. Enzyme defects often result in cell deaths in the nervous system and elsewhere. Other theories of aging blame simple wear and tear, suggesting that various physical and neural systems break down from frequent use, and may break down even faster if they are put under stress. Still other theories suggest that aging results from the accumulation of metabolic waste products in the cells or the increase in unstable chemicals (free radicals) that interact with molecules in the cells and interfere with their functioning.

Regardless of the reason for aging effects, the brain and nervous system of dogs (and people) change markedly as they age. Old dogs have smaller, lighter brains than young dogs have. The change is

quite significant; the older brain might be up to 25 percent lighter. It is important to note that this change is not necessarily due to brain cells dying off. Actually, we lose mostly parts of the nerve cells, specifically the branches (dendrites and axon filaments) that connect with other nerve cells. These connections to other cells start to break down with age. If we considered the brain as a complexly wired computer, it would be the same as if various circuits in the central processor simply stopped functioning because connections were broken. For the most part, it is the loss of these connections that reduces the size and the weight of the brain.

With age, chemical changes in the brain affect behavior, memory, and learning. In dogs and humans, the mitochondria, little strand-like structures in the nucleus of cells, are responsible for converting nutrients into energy. As dogs and humans age, mitochondrial efficiency decreases. The mitochondria begin to act as if they've become leaky, since they now begin to release "free radicals," chemicals that oxidize compounds essential for normal cell function. The loss of these compounds places the cell at risk. As the tissues degenerate, protein deposits called "amyloids" accumulate in the brain. High levels of amyloids, especially when associated with clusters of dead and dying nerve cells, are taken as part of the evidence that the individual is suffering from Alzheimer's disease. Studies conducted at the University of Toronto by a team of researchers including psychologist Norton Milgram have shown that dogs with high levels of amyloids in their brains have poorer memories and difficulties learning new material, especially if the learning process involves more complex thinking and problem solving. This equivalent to Alzheimer's disease in dogs is called *Canine Cognitive Dysfunction Syndrome*.

Physical evidence of this syndrome (found only in autopsies) reveals the same sort of degenerative brain lesions in dogs that occurs in humans with Alzheimer's disease. With age, dogs, like humans, naturally accumulate deposits of beta-amyloid. This starch-like protein builds up, becomes waxy, and forms plaque. As plaque builds up, it clogs the brain and inhibits the transmission of signals from the brain. In both Alzheimer's disease and Canine Cognitive Dysfunction Syndrome, the level of this accumulated plaque predicts the severity of the mental or cognitive impairment.

There are some noticeable changes in dogs with Canine Cognitive Dysfunction Syndrome that, as in Alzheimer's, are not a normal part of aging. The main symptoms can be easily summarized by the acronym DISH, which is short for "Disorientation, Interaction changes, Sleep changes, and House soiling."

Signs of disorientation often include the following:

- Some dogs stop responding to well-learned commands.
- Some dogs even stop responding to their own name.
- Some dogs no longer remember household routines.
- Some dogs stare blankly into space or at walls.
- Some dogs pace or wander aimlessly, and outside, they may wander out of their own yard and act lost or confused.
- Some dogs seem to walk in aimless repetitive patterns, such as around a table or from room to room.
- Some dogs appear lost or confused, even in familiar surroundings, and sometimes seem to get stuck in corners, under or behind furniture, and have difficulty finding their way out.
- Sometimes, previously well-tempered dogs appear to become easily agitated and bark a lot for no apparent reason.

Symptoms of decreased interaction skills include the following:

- In many dogs, the first thing you notice is that they no longer seem to care about being petted and may even walk away even when being petted and receiving affection.
- Previously sociable, affectionate dogs may no longer try to get attention.
- Some dogs no longer greet visitors or even family members.

Typical changes in sleep patterns include the following:

- Some dogs sleep more during the day.
- Some dogs sleep less at night and instead wander around in the dark.

Sometimes symptoms include apparently forgetting housebreaking:

- Some dogs stop signaling that they want to go out.
- Some dogs may begin to have "accidents" indoors. These accidents may even occur just a short time after the dog has been outside.
- Some dogs seem to forget the reason that they're outside, simply wandering around aimlessly and not eliminating.

The more of these symptoms the dog is showing, the more likely it is that he is suffering from Canine Cognitive Dysfunction Syndrome, the dog equivalent of Alzheimer's disease.

PART 6

What Else Does My Dog
Want Me to Know?

Are Dogs Just Tame Wolves?

MANY PEOPLE BELIEVE that dogs are simply domesticated wolves. This belief is maintained by the fact that some dogs look so much like wolves that it is difficult for anyone, except a trained scientist, to tell them apart. Examples of similarities like these are the German Shepherd Dog and the Timber Wolf, or the Siberian Husky and the Arctic Wolf. Of course, this argument is weakened by the fact that some dogs (like Dachshunds and Saint Bernards) look nothing at all like a wolf. So how do scientists decide whether dogs started out as wolves?

Many scientific procedures are available for attempting to answer these questions. One is to look at genetic material—namely, the DNA of dogs and wolves. When we do this, we find that on average there is a nearly 99 percent overlap between the DNA of wolves and domestic dogs. In fact the DNA of different breeds of dogs may sometimes differ from each other more than the DNA of certain older breeds differs from that of wolves.

Before these genetic similarities lead us to conclude that dogs and wolves must be the same species, differing only in the fact that dogs have been domesticated and tamed to coexist with humans, we must consider some other facts. First, both dogs and wolves belong

to the phylogenetic grouping Carnivora, or meat eaters. This group includes a large number of other canine species, including jackals, coyotes, dingoes, wild dogs, and foxes. Let's ignore the foxes for a moment, since the most common foxes (like the red fox) have the wrong number of chromosomes to be part of the dog's lineage, although some other varieties, such as the white Arctic Fox and black Niger Fox, might still be possibilities. When we look at the DNA from all of these other wild canine species and compare each to the DNA of domestic dogs, we find that they show the same range of overlap with dogs. This means that the DNA of a jackal or a dingo looks as much like the DNA of a dog as does the DNA of a wolf.

If the answer we get from the DNA is not conclusive, then perhaps we can use another technique. There is an alternative way of assessing whether two animals are the same species that has been accepted for a long time. It involves determining whether the two animals in question can interbreed. The ability of two test animals to interbreed and produce live, fertile offspring is usually accepted as evidence that they are of the same species. The fact that dogs and wolves can interbreed is well known. In fact, some people deliberately produce wolf-dog hybrids for sale on the open market as exotic pets. However, scientists have also shown that domestic dogs can successfully interbreed with jackals, coyotes, dingoes, African wild dogs, and the Arctic and Niger foxes as well.

We must remember, though, that physiology is not everything. We know, for example, that dogs and wolves behave differently. To mention just a few differences, wolves are active and able hunters, while many dog breeds have lost that talent. Wolves pace, dogs trot. Dogs bond easily with humans, while wolves do not. Dogs can be trained to respond to human commands reliably, while wolves, with some rare exceptions, cannot. In a wolf pack, only the most dominant individuals (usually referred to as the "alphas") lift their legs to urinate—even the alpha female will do this, though not necessarily all the time—while other pack members squat.

So what do we conclude from such data? It may be better to rephrase the question so that we can find an answer. Let's ask it this way: Which species are the ancestors of dogs? It appears likely that the first canine to be domesticated and thus become a dog was the gray wolf. However, the genetic data would suggest that perhaps the simplest and most conservative conclusion is that dogs are a genetic mixture of many of the existing wild canine species and perhaps even some that are now extinct. If such were the case, it would go a long way toward explaining how we have enough genetic variation in domestic dogs to produce breeds as different as Pekingese and Great Danes.

Are There More Wolves Than Dogs?

RIGHT NOW THE planet Earth is dominated by human beings. For an animal species to survive, it must not only successfully reproduce itself, but it must also get along with, and perhaps earn the protection of, humans. Given that fact, the answer to the question of whether there are more wolves than dogs should be obvious.

It is difficult to imagine that, except for humans, wolves were once the widest-ranging mammal on the planet. They could be found in the most extreme environments, from the heat of the desert to the frozen Arctic tundra. They were numerous on prairies and grasslands, as well as in forests and jungles. However, since wolves and humans competed for the same kinds of food—namely, meat—and wolves considered humans' domestic livestock fair game, humans have taken action against wolves. Over the past five hundred years humans have massively reduced the wolf populations. The British Isles have been without wolves for more than four hundred years, and many parts of western Europe have been virtually without wolves for several hundred years. The combined wolf population of France, Germany, and Italy is estimated to be under five hundred at the time of this writing.

In addition to the survival pressure put on wolves by humans, the typical wolf breeding pattern keeps their numbers low. In a wolf pack, only the pack leaders, the alpha male and the alpha female, typically breed. Wolves come into season only once a year, and the female seldom has her first litter until she is two or three years old. The average size of the litter is four to six pups. The mortality rate among wolf pups is typically about 50 percent, meaning that the average pack will increase in size by just two or three animals per year, which is only a little bit better than the rate needed to replace the number of pack members that die each year.

So the outcome is inevitable. Even if we add together all the wolf species from all the countries in the world, we get about 400,000 individual wolves, compared to 525 million dogs. In other words, for every wolf alive today there are more than 1,300 dogs living in the world.

How Many Dogs Are There in the World?

TO FIND OUT the exact number of dogs in the world is a task easier said than done, since in many countries people don't keep dogs inside their homes as pets. In some places dogs simply roam freely in the streets and nobody really owns them, which makes taking a count of them difficult and imprecise. The largest push to find out at least how many pet dogs there are has come from the pet food industry doing market research. This is a big industry, and in the United States alone consumers spend over $40 billion each year just on dog food. In the search to find out whether investing in this industry would be profitable in various parts of the world, a number of research groups have been employed to take a sort of census of pet dogs in target countries. The results that they've obtained are interesting, although incomplete.

As of this writing, approximately 42.5 million households in the United States own one or more dogs, and the total number of dogs in the country is in excess of 73 million. Their northern neighbor, Canada, has approximately 6 million pet dogs.

Western Europe has about 43 million pet dogs. The biggest pet dog populations in that region are in France, with 8.8 million, while Italy and Poland each have about 7.5 million, and the United Kingdom has 6.8 million pet dogs. In eastern Europe, Russia has about 12 million pet dogs, while the Ukraine has about 5.1 million.

The data from South America is spotty, and the only figures I could find were for Brazil (30 million pet dogs), Argentina (6.5 million), and Columbia (5 million). There are also many uncounted unregistered dogs in this region, especially outside of the larger metropolitan areas. The same holds for Australia, with 4 million recorded pet dogs, and perhaps half again as many strays or dogs that have become feral in the less settled regions of the country.

The statistics in Asia are not particularly reliable. Owned dogs do not have to be registered in China, but the number of pet dogs has been estimated to be 110 million. Even in the large cities that have dog registration regulations, many owners still refuse to get licenses for their pets, but some estimates peg the number of dogs in the capitol city of Beijing alone at more than 1 million. There is a similar problem in India, where many dogs are strays and unowned, and therefore are not counted. Here the best estimate is that there

are approximately 32 million owned dogs and perhaps as many as 20 million stray dogs. The Japanese, by contrast, seem to be quite conscientious in registering their pets, and the number of recorded pet dogs in Japan is 9.5 million.

Perhaps the most difficult place to get statistics on the dog population is Africa. While the nation of South Africa provides data suggesting that there are 9 million pet dogs in its boundaries, the information from the rest of the continent is sparse. The World Health Organization, which tries to monitor the dog population on this continent because of the impact of rabies on humans, estimates that there are about 78 million owned dogs in Africa, but that there may be in excess of 70 million unowned, stray dogs as well.

If we roughly total all of these estimates, our best guess is that there are at least 525 million dogs on our planet. That number is the equivalent of all the people in the United States, Canada, Great Britain, Germany, Italy, and France combined!

Why Are There So Many Dogs in the World?

WHEN CHARLES DARWIN talked about survival of the fittest, he was not talking about survival of the biggest and strongest species. He was really talking about survival of those species that are most successful in reproducing and having their offspring survive to reproduce. He would tell you that the measure of the success of a species is how many individuals are alive and reproducing. To achieve this success the individuals have to "fit" into their particular environment.

The environment that dogs live in is the same environment that humans live in. Thus, dogs succeed as a species to the extent that they fit into our niche in the world. It turns out that dogs have done very well in this task. They fit into our lives so well that we feed them, care for them, and attend to their health and medical needs to such a degree that they live long lives and many of them do have the opportunity to breed. Furthermore, dogs have no natural predators (although automobiles and trucks may serve as a stand-in for that function in areas where dogs are allowed to run free).

Since breeding and reproduction are the measures of success, it is interesting to note that as a by-product of our domestication of dogs, we have changed their breeding pattern in a major way.

Among wild canines, such as wolves, females come into season (that is, ovulate and become fertile) only once each year. Except for a few of the more primitive breeds (such as the Basenji), dogs come into season twice a year, thus allowing them to produce twice as many offspring as their wild cousins do.

Now the stage is set to explain why the dog population is so large. We start off with the fact that a female dog can have her first litter of puppies when she is only five to eighteen months old (depending on her breed). It takes fifty-eight to sixty-five days to give birth to the puppies. The number of pups in a litter varies with the breed and size of the dog, but the overall average ranges between six and ten pups. Most female dogs can have two batches of puppies each year. If half of these puppies are females, they can also have pups starting when they are five to eighteen months old. Do the math, and you will find that one female dog and her children can potentially produce 4,372 puppies in seven years! Male dogs don't even have the limitation of two batches of puppies a year, since they can sire a litter whenever a female in heat is available.

The downside of all this is that dogs are actually too successful, and in some places they are suffering from overpopulation. Most people don't seem to understand the size of the overpopulation problem. In the United States, for example, between four and six million dogs are euthanized each year simply because there's no one to adopt them and no room at animal shelters. So, in effect, humans have become agents of natural selection who keep the populations of dogs in check.

What Is a Hound?

HOUNDS ARE AMONG the oldest groups of dogs we know of. Actually, the very word "hound" tells us the function of this type of dog. Hounds have been bred to chase or hound a quarry by using their sense of smell or sight, or a combination of both. The antiquity of this type of dog is demonstrated by the fact that pictures of hounds on the hunt appear on the walls of pyramids and temples in ancient Egypt and Assyria.

There are two classes of hounds, named according to their dominant sense: *scent hounds* and *sight hounds*. The major task of "scent hounds" is to find animals and track them using their sense of smell. "Sight hounds," sometimes called "gaze hounds," have the job of sighting their quarry and chasing it down.

Sight hounds are specialized animals that have been bred to have exceptional eyesight and also the speed and stamina needed to chase and catch their intended prey once they've spotted it. The sight hounds are therefore among the fastest of all of the dogs, and they include Greyhounds, Salukis, and Afghan Hounds, which are all older breeds from North Africa and the Middle East, where they were used to hunt fleet-footed antelope and gazelle.

Scent hounds specialize in following the scent, or smell, of their quarry using their sensitive noses. Speed and keen eyesight are of less importance to animals such as these. While all dogs have a good sense of smell, some scent hounds have been specifically bred so that their sense of smell is astonishing. The Bloodhound has the keenest sense of smell of any of the hounds or any other breed of dog. The tiny Beagle, which is one of the smallest of the hounds, has a nose that is much more sensitive than that of many dog breeds that are larger and should have larger noses. This is one reason why the Beagle is favored as the animal to sniff out contraband food and agricultural products in airports, and even to detect things like termites, bedbugs, or various toxic molds that may end up in human homes and other buildings.

Because hounds were developed well before the advent of firearms or even bows and arrows, they were bred to do much of their hunting on their own, with little human guidance. If the prey was small, the hunter's task was simply to catch up and recover it after

the hounds had killed it and before they had eaten it. If the prey was large, the hounds were expected to hold the animal at bay until the hunters could arrive with their spears, clubs, or axes to kill it. For this reason, hounds are relatively independent dogs. Although many hounds have sweet and calm dispositions, they are not particularly attentive to human beings. Because they lack the attention focused on humans that other breeds such as retrievers, herding, and working dogs have, it is thus not surprising that hounds are among the most difficult dogs to train. In research that ranked dogs on the basis of their working and obedience intelligence (which is really a measure of a dog's trainability), six of the bottom ten ranked are hounds. This does not mean that hounds are stupid, but that they were specifically bred to work alone, with little need of guidance from, or obedience to, their human masters.

Which Are the Heaviest, Lightest, Tallest, Shortest Dogs?

I F ALIEN BIOLOGISTS ever landed on Earth and began classifying animals, I doubt they would decide that the Newfoundland, Dachshund, and Chihuahua were the same species. There is an incredible amount of variation in the shapes and sizes of dogs. Evidence suggests that dogs exhibit the greatest amount of variation in size of any single mammalian species. For example, the heaviest and longest dog recorded in the last 150 years was a Tibetan Mastiff named Chloe. This dog weighed 365 pounds (165 kilograms). She also measured 8 feet 5 inches (260 centimeters) from her nose to her tail tip. Contrast this animal to a Yorkshire Terrier named Sylvia, owned by Arthur Marples of Blackburn, England. Sylvia is believed to be the smallest dog ever recorded. She lived to be only two years old, and when she died she was only 2½ inches (6½ centimeters) tall at the shoulder and stretched only 3¾ inches (9½ centimeters) from nose to root of the tail, which made Sylvia about the same size as a box of kitchen matches. Sylvia weighed a bit less than 4 ounces (110 grams), about as much as a quarter pound hamburger—without the bun!

Generally speaking, the heaviest dog (considering the average weight of the male dog) today is the English Mastiff, which weighs

in at 175–220 pounds (80–100 kilograms). English Mastiffs are actually a miniaturized version of an ancient war dog called the Molossian Dog which could grow to 325 pounds (120 kilograms).

The tallest dog breed, on average, is the Irish Wolfhound, which stands about 33 inches (84 centimeters) at the shoulder. However, the tallest dog recorded in recent history was a Great Dane named Gibson, who was about 42 inches (107 centimeters) at the shoulder and stretched to nearly 7 feet (210 centimeters) tall when standing on his hind legs.

The shortest and smallest dog, on average, is the Chihuahua, which stands only 8 inches (20 centimeters) tall at the shoulder and weighs only about 6 pounds (2.7 kilograms). Many Yorkshire Terriers are in that same height and weight range, but some are considerably larger, raising the breed's average height and weight.

Scientists have tried to determine why the size of our domestic dogs varies so much. One recent study looked at the DNA of the

Portuguese Water Dog. The researchers chose this breed because it contains a broad range of sizes, from around 16 to 23 inches (41–50 centimeters) at the shoulder. What they found was that variations in a single gene determined the dog's size. This gene is the gene that codes for "insulin growth factor 1" (IGF1). The size of any given Portuguese Water Dog was predicted by which variation of the IGF1 gene the dog had. The researchers then extended the study to look at the DNA of over thirty-two hundred dogs. Surprisingly, these new genetic samples were obtained from a database owned by the Mars candy company. Mars also makes pet food, and it has accumulated and maintained the largest gene bank of canine DNA in the world. This second analysis confirmed that the size difference between dogs of different breeds is controlled by variations of this same gene.

How Many Dog Breeds Are There?

T HE *WORLD CANINE Organisation* is best known by its French name, Fédération Cynologique Internationale, which is abbreviated FCI. It is the largest registry of dog breeds that is internationally accepted. At the time of this writing, the FCI recognizes 339 breeds of dogs, which are divided into ten groups based on the dog's purpose or function, or on its appearance or size. The ten groups are

1. Sheepdogs and cattle dogs other than Swiss cattle dogs (this group includes most of the dogs found classified as "herding dogs" by other kennel clubs)
2. Pinscher and Schnauzer, Molossoid breeds, Swiss mountain and cattle dogs, and other breeds (the Molossoid breeds include the dogs known as the mastiffs by most other kennel clubs)
3. Terriers
4. Dachshunds
5. Spitz and primitive types
6. Scent hounds and related breeds
7. Pointers and setters
8. Retrievers, flushing dogs, and water dogs
9. Companion and toy dogs
10. Sight hounds

Each group is divided into subgroups of dog breeds, and each has been assigned a country of origin, as the accompanying table indicates. While the country listed may not be the very first place where the dog breed appears, it is usually the first nation to have recognized and registered the breed, and it is currently the home of the breed organization that determines the breed's "standard" (the description of the ideal qualities of a dog of that particular breed). You will probably find some surprises in this list, such as the fact that the Australian Shepherd is actually a breed created in the United States, while the Pharaoh Hound was not developed in Egypt, but in Malta. You will also find that France, Germany, and Great Britain are responsible for creating more dog breeds than nearly the rest of the world combined.

DOG BREEDS RECOGNIZED BY THE WORLD CANINE ORGANISATION

AFGHANISTAN
Afghan Hound (long-haired sight
   hound)

ANATOLIA
Anatolian Shepherd Dog (mountain-
   type mastiff)

ARGENTINA
Dogo Argentino (mastiff)

AUSTRALIA
Australian Cattle Dog (cattle dog)
Australian Kelpie (sheepdog)
Australian Silky Terrier (toy terrier)
Australian Stumpy Tail Cattle Dog
   (cattle dog)
Australian Terrier (small terrier)
Jack Russell Terrier (small terrier)

AUSTRIA
Alpine Dachsbracke (leash hound)
Austrian Black and Tan Hound
   (medium scent hound)
Austrian Pinscher (pinscher)
Styrian Coarse-haired Hound
   (medium scent hound)
Tyrolean Hound (medium scent
   hound)

BELGIUM
Belgian Sheepdog (4 varieties)
   Groenendael (sheepdog)
   Laekenois (sheepdog)

   Malinois (sheepdog)
   Tervueren (sheepdog)
Bloodhound (large scent hound)
Griffon Belge (companion/toy dog)
Griffon Bruxellois (companion/toy
   dog)
Petit Brabançon (companion/toy
   dog)

BOSNIA
Bosnian Coarse-haired Hound
   (medium scent hound)

BRAZIL
Fila Brasileiro (mastiff)

CANADA
Newfoundland (mountain-type
   mastiff)
Nova Scotia Duck Tolling Retriever
   (retriever)

CENTRAL AFRICA
Basenji (primitive type)

CENTRAL MEDITERRANEAN
Maltese (companion/toy dog)

CHINA
Chinese Crested Dog (2 varieties)
   Hairless (companion/toy dog)
   Powderpuff (companion/toy
      dog)
Chow Chow (Asian spitz)

Pekingese (companion/toy dog)
Shar Pei (mastiff)

CROATIA

Croatian Sheepdog (sheepdog)
Dalmatian (scent hound)
Istrian Hound (2 varieties)
    Coarse-haired (medium scent
      hound)
    Short-haired (medium scent
      hound)
Posavaz Hound (medium scent
    hound)

CZECHOSLOVAKIA

Ceský Fousek (griffon-type pointer)
Ceský Terrier (small terrier)
Czechoslovakian Wolfdog (sheep-
    dog)

DENMARK

Broholmer (mastiff)
Old Danish Pointer (continental
    pointing dog)

FINLAND

Finnish Hound (medium scent
    hound)
Finnish Lapphund (Nordic watch-
    dog/herding dog)
Finnish Spitz (Nordic hunting dog)
Karelian Bear Dog (Nordic hunting
    dog)
Lapponian Herder (Nordic watch-
    dog/herding dog)

FRANCE

Anglo-Français de Petite Vénerie
    (medium scent hound)
Ariégeois (medium scent hound)
Barbet (water dog)
Basset Artésien Normand (small
    scent hound)
Basset Bleu de Gascogne (small
    scent hound)
Basset Fauve de Bretagne (small
    scent hound)
Beagle-Harrier (medium scent
    hound)
Beauceron (sheepdog)
Berger Picard (sheepdog)
Bichon Frise (companion/toy dog)
Billy (large scent hound)
Bouvier des Ardennes (cattle dog)
Bouvier des Flandres (cattle dog)
Braque d'Auvergne (continental
    pointing dog)
Braque de l'Ariège (continental
    pointing dog)
Braque du Bourbonnais (continental
    pointing dog)
Braque Français, type Gascogne
    (continental pointing dog)
Braque Français, type Pyrénées
    (continental pointing dog)
Braque Saint-Germain (continental
    pointing dog)
Briard (sheepdog)
Briquet Griffon Vendéen (medium
    scent hound)
Brittany Spaniel (spaniel-type
    pointer)

Chien d'Artois (medium scent hound)

Epagneul Bleu de Picardie (spaniel-type pointer)

Epagneul de Picardie (spaniel-type pointer)

Epagneul Français (spaniel-type pointer)

Epagneul Pont-Audemer (spaniel-type pointer)

Français Blanc et Noir (large scent hound)

Français Blanc et Orange (large scent hound)

Français Tricolore (large scent hound)

French Bulldog (companion/toy dog)

Gascon Saintongeois (medium scent hound)

Grand Anglo-Français Blanc et Noir (large scent hound)

Grand Anglo-Français Blanc et Orange (large scent hound)

Grand Anglo-Français Tricolore (large scent hound)

Grand Basset Griffon Vendéen (small scent hound)

Grand Bleu de Gascogne (large scent hound)

Grand Gascon Saintongeois (large scent hound)

Grand Griffon Vendéen (large scent hound)

Griffon Bleu de Gascogne (medium scent hound)

Griffon Fauve de Bretagne (medium scent hound)

Griffon Nivernais (medium scent hound)

Lowchen (companion/toy dog)

Papillon (companion/toy dog)

Petit Basset Griffon Vendéen (small scent hound)

Petit Bleu de Gascogne (medium scent hound)

Phalene (companion/toy dog)

Poitevin (large scent hound)

Poodle (4 varieties)

    Standard (companion/toy dog)

    Medium (companion/toy dog)

    Miniature (companion/toy dog)

    Toy (companion/toy dog)

Porcelaine (medium scent hound)

Pyrenean Mountain Dog (mountain-type mastiff)

Pyrenean Shepherd (sheepdog)

Wirehaired Pointing Griffon (griffon-type pointer)

GERMANY

Affenpinscher (pinscher)

Bavarian Mountain Hound (leash hound)

Boxer (mastiff)

Deutscher Jagdterrier (German Hunting Terrier)

Doberman Pinscher (pinscher)

Eurasia (Asian spitz)

German Hound (small scent hound)

German Longhaired Pointer (spaniel-type pointer)

German Pinscher (pinscher)
German Shepherd Dog (sheepdog)
German Shorthaired Pointer
   (continental pointing dog)
German Spaniel (flushing dog)
German Spitz (3 varieties)
   Grossspitz (large European
      spitz)
   Mittelspitz (medium European
      spitz)
   Kleinspitz (small European
      spitz)
German Wirehaired Pointer
   (continental pointing dog)
Giant Schnauzer (schnauzer)
Great Dane (mastiff)
Hanover Hound (leash hound)
Hovawart (mountain-type mastiff)
Keeshond (European spitz)
Kromfohrländer (companion/toy
   dog)
Landseer (mountain-type mastiff)
Large Munsterlander (spaniel-type
   pointer)
Leonberger (mountain-type mastiff)
Miniature Dachshund (3 varieties)
   Smooth-haired (dachshund)
   Wire-haired (dachshund)
   Long-haired (dachshund)
Miniature Pinscher (pinscher)
Miniature Schnauzer (schnauzer)
Pomeranian (European spitz)
Pudelpointer (continental pointing
   dog)
Rabbit Dachshund (3 varieties)
   Smooth-haired (dachshund)

Wire-haired (dachshund)
   Long-haired (dachshund)
Rottweiler (mastiff)
Small Munsterlander (spaniel-type
   pointer)
Standard Dachshund (3 varieties)
   Smooth-haired (dachshund)
   Wire-haired (dachshund)
   Long-haired (dachshund)
Standard Schnauzer (schnauzer)
Weimaraner (continental pointing
   dog)
Westphalian Dachsbracke (small
   scent hound)

GREAT BRITAIN

Airedale Terrier (large/medium
   terrier)
Basset Hound (small scent hound)
Beagle (small scent hound)
Bearded Collie (sheepdog)
Bedlington Terrier (large/medium
   terrier)
Border Collie (sheepdog)
Border Terrier (large/
   medium terrier)
Bull Terrier (2 varieties)
   Miniature (bull-type terrier)
   Standard (bull-type terrier)
Bulldog (mastiff)
Bullmastiff (mastiff)
Cairn Terrier (small terrier)
Cardigan Welsh Corgi (sheepdog)
Cavalier King Charles Spaniel
   (companion/toy dog)
Clumber Spaniel (flushing dog)

Curly Coated Retriever (retriever)

Dandie Dinmont Terrier (small terrier)

Deerhound (rough-haired sight hound)

English Cocker Spaniel (flushing dog)

English Foxhound (large scent hound)

English Mastiff (mastiff)

English Pointer (pointer)

English Setter (setter)

English Springer Spaniel (flushing dog)

English Toy Terrier (Black and Tan) (toy terrier)

Field Spaniel (flushing dog)

Flat Coated Retriever (retriever)

Fox Terrier (2 varieties)

    Smooth (large/medium sized terrier)

    Wire (large/medium sized terrier)

Golden Retriever (retriever)

Gordon Setter (setter)

Greyhound (short-haired sight hound)

Harrier (medium scent hound)

King Charles Spaniel (companion/ toy dog)

Labrador Retriever (retriever)

Lakeland Terrier (large/medium terrier)

Manchester Terrier (large/medium terrier)

Norfolk Terrier (small terrier)

Norwich Terrier (small terrier)

Old English Sheepdog (sheepdog)

Otterhound (large scent hound)

Parson Russell Terrier (large/ medium terrier)

Pembroke Welsh Corgi (sheepdog)

Pug (companion/toy dog)

Rough Collie (sheepdog)

Scottish Terrier (small terrier)

Sealyham Terrier (small terrier)

Shetland Sheepdog (sheepdog)

Skye Terrier (small terrier)

Smooth Collie (sheepdog)

Staffordshire Bull Terrier (bull-type terrier)

Sussex Spaniel (flushing dog)

Welsh Springer Spaniel (flushing dog)

Welsh Terrier (large/medium terrier)

West Highland White Terrier (small terrier)

Whippet (short-haired sight hound)

Yorkshire Terrier (toy terrier)

GREECE

Hellenic Hound (medium scent hound)

GREENLAND

Greenland Dog (Nordic sledge dog)

HUNGARY

Hungarian Greyhound (short-haired sight hound)

Hungarian Vizsla (2 varieties)

Shorthaired (continental
pointing dog)
Wirehaired (continental
pointing dog)
Komondor (sheepdog)
Kuvasz (sheepdog)
Mudi (sheepdog)
Puli (sheepdog)
Pumi (sheepdog)
Transylvanian Hound (medium
scent hound)

ICELAND
Icelandic Sheepdog (Nordic
watchdog/herding dog)

IRELAND
Irish Glen of Imaal Terrier (large/
medium terrier)
Irish Red and White Setter (setter)
Irish Setter (setter)
Irish Terrier (large/medium terrier)
Irish Water Spaniel (water dog)
Irish Wolfhound (rough-haired sight
hound)
Kerry Blue Terrier (large/medium
terrier)
Soft-Coated Wheaten Terrier (large/
medium terrier)

ISRAEL
Canaan Dog (primitive type)

ITALY
Bergamasco (sheepdog)
Bolognese (companion/toy dog)

Bracco Italiano (continental
pointing dog)
Cane Corso Italiano (mastiff)
Cirneco dell'Etna (primitive type/
hunting dog)
Italian Greyhound (short-haired
sight hound)
Lagotto Romagnolo (water dog)
Maremma Sheepdog (sheepdog)
Neapolitan Mastiff (mastiff)
Segugio Italiano (medium scent
hound)
Spinone Italiano (griffon-type
pointer)
Volpino Italiano (European spitz)

JAPAN
Akita (Asian spitz)
American Akita (Asian spitz)
Hokkaido (Asian spitz)
Japanese Chin (companion/toy dog)
Japanese Spitz (Asian spitz)
Japanese Terrier (Nihon Teria)
(small terrier)
Kai (Asian spitz)
Kishu (Asian spitz)
Shiba (Asian spitz)
Shikoku (Asian spitz)
Tosa Inu (mastiff)

KOREA
Korean Jindo (Asian spitz)

MADAGASCAR
Coton de Tuléar (companion/toy
dog)

MALI
Azawakh (short-haired sight hound)

MALTA
Pharaoh Hound (primitive type)

MEXICO
Chihuahua (2 varieties)
  Shorthaired (companion/toy
    dog)
  Longhaired (companion/toy
    dog)
Mexican Hairless Dog (primitive
  type)

MIDDLE EAST
Saluki (long-haired sight hound)

MONTENEGRO
Montenegrin Mountain Hound
  (medium scent hound)

MOROCCO
Aidi (mountain-type mastiff)
Sloughi (Arabian Greyhound)
  (short-haired sight hound)

NETHERLANDS
Dutch Partridge Dog (spaniel-type
  pointer)
Dutch Schapendoes (sheepdog)
Dutch Shepherd Dog (sheepdog)
Dutch Smoushond (smoushond)
Kooikerhondje (flushing dog)
Saarloos Wolfdog (sheepdog)
Stabyhoun (spaniel-type pointer)

Wetterhoun (water dog)

NORWAY
Black Norwegian Elkhound (Nordic
  hunting dog)
Dunker (medium scent hound)
Haldenstøvare (medium scent
  hound)
Hygenhund (medium scent hound)
Norwegian Buhund (Nordic
  watchdog/herding dog)
Norwegian Elkhound (Nordic
  hunting dog)
Norwegian Lundehund (Nordic
  hunting dog)

PERU
Peruvian Hairless Dog (primitive
  type)

POLAND
Chart Polski (Polish Greyhound)
  (short-haired sight hound)
Polish Hound (medium scent hound)
Polish Lowland Sheepdog (sheep-
  dog)
Tatra Shepherd Dog (sheepdog)

PORTUGAL
Cão Fila de São Miguel (mastiff)
Castro Laboreiro Dog (mountain-
  type mastiff)
Estrela Mountain Dog (mountain-
  type mastiff)
Podengo Português (primitive type/
  hunting dog)

Portuguese Pointer (continental pointing dog)

Portuguese Sheepdog (sheepdog)

Portuguese Water Dog (water dog)

Rafeiro of Alentejo (mountain-type mastiff)

RUSSIA

Borzoi (long-haired sight hound)

Caucasian Shepherd Dog (mountain-type mastiff)

Central Asia Shepherd Dog (mountain-type mastiff)

East Siberian Laika (Nordic hunting dog)

Russo-European Laika (Nordic hunting dog)

Samoyed (Nordic sledge dog)

South Russian Shepherd Dog (sheepdog)

West Siberian Laika (Nordic hunting dog)

SERBIA

Illyrian Shepherd Dog (mountain-type mastiff)

Serbian Hound (medium scent hound)

Serbian Tricolour Hound (medium scent hound)

SLOVAKIA

Slovakian Chuvach (sheepdog)

Slovakian Hound (medium scent hound)

Slovenský Hrubosrsty Stavac (griffon-type pointer)

Tchiorny Terrier (large/medium terrier)

SLOVENIA

Karst Shepherd Dog (mountain-type mastiff)

SPAIN

Ca de Bou (mastiff)

Catalan Sheepdog (sheepdog)

Dogo Canario (mastiff)

Majorca Shepherd Dog (sheepdog)

Podenco Canario (primitive type/hunting dog)

Podenco Ibicenco (primitive type/hunting dog)

Pyrenean Mastiff (mountain-type mastiff)

Spanish Greyhound (short-haired sight hound)

Spanish Hound (medium scent hound)

Spanish Mastiff (mountain-type mastiff)

Spanish Pointer (continental pointing dog)

Spanish Water Dog (water dog)

SWEDEN

Drever (small scent hound)

Hamiltonstövare (medium scent hound)

Norrbottenspets (Nordic hunting dog)

Schillerstövare (medium scent
hound)
Smålandsstövare (medium scent
hound)
Swedish Elkhound (Nordic hunting
dog)
Swedish Lapphund (Nordic
watchdog/herding dog)
Swedish Vallhund (Nordic watch-
dog/herding dog)

SWITZERLAND
Appenzeller Mountain Dog (Swiss
mountain dog)
Bernese Mountain Dog (Swiss
mountain dog)
Entlebucher Mountain Dog (Swiss
mountain dog)
Greater Swiss Mountain Dog (Swiss
mountain dog)
Saint Bernard (mountain-type
mastiff)
Small Swiss Hound (4 varieties)
   Small Bernese Hound (small
      scent hound)
   Small Jura Hound (small scent
      hound)
   Small Lucerne Hound (small
      scent hound)
   Small Schwyz Hound (small
      scent hound)
Swiss Hound (4 varieties)
   Bernese Hound (medium scent
      hound)
   Jura Hound (medium scent
      hound)

Lucerne Hound (medium scent
hound)
Schwyz Hound (medium scent
hound)

THAILAND
Thai Ridgeback (primitive type/
ridgeback)

TIBET
Lhasa Apso (companion/toy
dog)
Shih Tzu (companion/toy dog)
Tibetan Mastiff (mountain-type
mastiff)
Tibetan Spaniel (companion/toy
dog)
Tibetan Terrier (companion/toy
dog)

UNITED STATES OF AMERICA
Alaskan Malamute (Nordic sledge
dog)
American Cocker Spaniel (flushing
dog)
American Foxhound (large scent
hound)
American Staffordshire Terrier
(bull-type terrier)
American Water Spaniel (water
dog)
Australian Shepherd (sheepdog)
Black and Tan Coonhound (large
scent hound)
Boston Terrier (companion/
toy dog)

Chesapeake Bay Retriever (retriever)

Siberian Husky (Nordic sledge dog)

Toy Fox Terrier (toy terrier)

WESTERN MEDITERRANEAN

Havanese (companion/toy dog)

ZIMBABWE

Rhodesian Ridgeback (primitive
type/ridgeback)

Note: This list is based on the nomenclature provided by the Fédération Cynologique Internationale (http://www.fci.be), the World Canine Organisation.

Could Dogs Be the Fastest Land Animals in the World?

T O DETERMINE THE fastest animal in the world, you must consider the nature of the race that you're going to ask the animal to run. If you were running an air race with level flight, the champion would be the swift, which can fly at 106 miles per hour (mph) (171 kilometers per hour [kph]). Peregrine falcons are slower but can reach speeds up to 69 mph (112 kph) in direct pursuit of prey, but when diving they can reach the incredible speed of 242 mph (389 kph), which would easily allow them to catch a fleeing swift. For a water race, the sailfish blows the competition away. Its streamlined body allows it to travel up to 68 mph (109 kph), and the swordfish can do around 60 mph (97 kph).

When we're talking about speed on land, however, the most important consideration is the distance over which the race is run. Much as in human track competitions, the shorter, sprint races will produce the fastest times. Participants in the longer races can't sustain the speed attained in shorter runs. Looking simply at the peak speed an animal can reach, we find, as most people already know, that the fastest land animal is the cheetah, which can reach 70 mph (113 kph). Although the cheetah is an astonishingly fast runner, it can maintain that incredible velocity for only about 200–300 yards

(274 meters), or less than two-tenths of a mile. Since these high speeds only allow the cat to overtake its prey within short distances, cheetahs must still rely on stealth, sneaking, and the element of surprise to get close enough to the gazelle before giving chase.

The fastest of horses is also a sprinter. It is the quarter horse, which gets its name from the fact that it was typically run in quarter-mile-long (0.4-kilometer) races. It can reach 47.5 mph (76 kph) over that distance, but it has pretty much burned out by the half-mile (0.8-kilometer) mark. Over a longer distance, horses are considerably slower than this peak value. When the thoroughbred race horse Secretariat set the Kentucky Derby speed record in 1973, he ran it at 38 mph (61 kph) over a distance of 1.5 miles (2.4 kilometers).

Humans have changed dogs so that some dogs can run much faster than most other animals. The really fast dogs are Greyhounds, Whippets, Salukis, and Afghan Hounds, which are called "sight hounds" because their job is to spot their quarry by sight and run it down. Characteristically, these dogs have a huge chest to accommodate large lungs to gulp oxygen and an oversized heart, plus a narrow waist that allows them to bend their body so that every stride carries them more than a body length.

The fastest of these dogs is the Greyhound. Greyhounds are specially designed for sustained, high-speed running. While going at full tilt, the dog's heart rate can rise to 300–360 beats per minute. This means that the Greyhound heart can contract and refill

with blood five times per second during a race, allowing oxygen to be transported at a phenomenal rate to supply the needs of the muscles. The Greyhound's ability to reach top speed quickly is amazing. At maximum acceleration, a Greyhound can reach a speed of 45 mph (72 kph) within its first six strides from a standing start. No other land animal (except the cheetah) has that degree of acceleration.

To give you an idea of how fast a sprinter the Greyhound is, compare its performance to that of an elite human runner. When Asafa Powell set his 100-meter world record, he was running at a speed of 22.9 mph (36.9 kph) and covered that distance in 9.77 seconds. A Greyhound would complete that same race in 5.33 seconds.

However, the Greyhound is also a distance runner. Greyhounds can settle into a speed in excess of 35 mph (56 kph) and can run at that rate for distances as long as 7 miles (11 kilometers). This means that while the cheetah can win the short sprint race, in any long race the Greyhound will leave that big cat way behind, panting in the dust.

Some dogs do even better in supermarathon races. For this we need a different type of dog, though. Consider the sled dogs, particularly Siberian Huskies, like those that participate in the Iditarod. This Alaskan sled race goes from just outside Anchorage to Nome, covering a distance of 1,161 miles (1,868 kilometers). The dog teams in this race run up to 125 miles (201 kilometers) per day, often racing for up to six hours at a time, for nine to fourteen days, pulling a sled weighing over 220 pounds (100 kilograms). Furthermore, they run at full tilt in extremes of climate where the windchill can be –100°F (–73.3°C). The record for the Iditarod race is currently eight days and twenty-two hours. A sled dog's typical racing pace averages 10–12 mph (16–19 kph), which means that in every six-hour running period he covers about 70 miles (112 kilometers). These dogs keep this up for an average of eleven days! It is hard to imagine any other animal on land that could keep up that kind of pace.

Do Dogs Sweat?

WHEN HUMANS' BODY temperature builds up, either because they're in a hot environment or because they've been exercising or working a great deal, they begin to perspire. When people sweat, it's fairly obvious. Everybody perspires, although some do more than others. For some people, sweat is visible only under their arms and on their brows; other people seem to sweat almost everywhere.

Sweating is one of the ways that our body regulates its temperature. Human sweat glands are distributed over most of the body's surface. When our internal temperature rises to an unhealthy level, sweat provides a slick of moisture over the skin that then begins to evaporate. As a fluid evaporates, it cools, and in that way sweat helps to lower our body temperature by effectively wrapping us in a thin, cool layer.

A dog's skin is quite different, which is why you have never seen a dog with sweaty underarms. Most of the dog's sweat glands are located around its foot pads. That's why, when a dog is overheated, you will sometimes see a trail of wet footprints that he has left behind as he walked across the floor.

Rather than sweating, the principal mechanism a dog uses to

cool himself is to pant with his mouth open. Panting allows the moisture on the dog's tongue to evaporate, and the heavy breathing allows the moist lining of the lungs to serve as a surface from which moisture can evaporate. In this way the dog can significantly lower his body temperature.

Another mechanism that dogs use to cool off involves dilating or expanding blood vessels in their face and ears. If it's not too hot outside, this blood vessel action helps to cool the dog's blood by causing it to flow closer to the surface of the skin. This mechanism works best if the overheating is due to exercise, rather than to a high outside temperature.

You might guess that another reason why dogs might not deal well with heat is that they are covered in fur, which could make their bodies quite hot in the summer. This is only partially the case, since fur is actually an insulator that serves as a barrier between the outside environment and the dog's interior. Fur acts much like the vacuum barrier in a thermos: In winter, it preserves body heat and

serves as a barrier to keep the cold out. In summer, it is a barrier to the outside heat. Unfortunately, in a continually hot environment, once the body temperature has risen, fur serves as an impediment to cooling, since the heat then has a hard time dissipating through it.

On a hot day, especially at high levels of activity, a dog can over-heat—a condition known as "hyperthermia." Hyperthermia can eventually lead to heat stroke. A dog that is overheated will seem sluggish and perhaps confused. If you look at his gums and tongue, they may appear bright red, and he will probably be panting very hard. If left unattended, the dog may collapse, have a seizure, or even go into a coma.

A simple trick that many dog owners use to help keep their pets cool on a hot day involves using a spray bottle or mister, such as those used on plants. Simply fill it with water and periodically spray your dog's body with it. In effect, you are creating a slick of moisture covering your dog, and it will evaporate and have the same cooling effect as if your dog had sweat glands all over his body.

Why Do Dogs Sometimes Sleep on Their Backs?

M OST DOG OWNERS have seen their dog occasionally sleeping on its back. This position is memorable because it appears so unstable and awkward that it's often comical. The reason that dogs adopt this position has to do with temperature control.

Dogs, especially those with long or double coats, are very good at conserving body heat. That's why northern dog breeds, such as the Alaskan Malamute, Samoyed, or Siberian Husky, can safely sleep outside in the snow at Arctic temperatures. The problem that dogs have is dissipating heat from the body when it becomes too hot. Since dogs do not sweat, except through the pads of their feet, their only other response to higher temperatures is panting, which cools the body a bit by evaporation of moisture from the tongue. Panting, however, is an active process and would run counter to the relaxation needed for sleep.

Dogs have another strategy for reducing their internal heat level. The fur on the dog's underside is considerably thinner and often is almost completely absent. That means that, by lying on his back, the dog exposes the least insulated portion of his body to the open air, thereby allowing some of his body heat to escape more easily. This can be an effective way to prevent overheating.

Dogs will also opportunistically use the environment to help reduce their internal temperature on hot days. Obviously, seeking a place in the shade helps. Some dogs will lie down in places where they can catch the air flowing from a fan. If you have a room with a ceramic tile floor, dogs may once again use the fact that the insulation is thinner on their underside. In this case, however, they tend to lie down on the floor with their belly directly against the cool tile and their limbs spread. This is also a comical pose, since it makes them look much like the pelt of a beaver or otter that has been spread out to dry.

Sometimes puppies sleep on their back for a different reason. From the time they are fully mobile until they are three or four months old, puppies act much like windup toys. It is amusing to watch them run and go full tilt and then, like a windup toy, simply stop. When they do stop, they may wobble, stagger, and virtually seem to topple over like felled trees. So in the case of puppies, it is not necessarily that they choose to sleep on their backs; it's just that when puppies run out of energy, they will sleep in whatever position or location they happen to be in at the time.

Why Do Dogs Have Dewclaws?

D EWCLAWS ARE SHORT claws or nails on the side of the foot that don't touch the ground. Most dogs have dewclaws only on their front paws, and it is rare to find them on their back paws. In several breeds, however, such as the Great Pyrenees and the Briard, rear dewclaws are common. The Great Pyrenees even has a double dewclaw, an inherited trait called "polydactyly," so that there are two bony digits instead of one.

For most dogs the dewclaws are nonfunctional, but they are an interesting bit of evidence of the distant evolutionary past of the species. Some 40 million years ago, there was a tree-climbing cat-like animal known as *Miacis*. Obviously, if you climb trees, having five toes is an advantage. However, *Miacis* eventually evolved into the ground-dwelling species *Cynodictis*. From this point on, successive generations of the animals that would become our dogs began to become specialized as social hunters. Because they were hunting fast-moving prey, speed became an important factor. Today's dogs are a "cursorial" species, which means that evolution has adapted them to be swift runners. To obtain the added speed required a change in canine physiology.

Animals like humans and bears are "plantigrade" species, which means that they place the full length of their foot on the ground during each stride and then move with a rolling action that goes from heel to toe. While this mode of walking gives good balance and stability, it is a relatively slow process. What evolution did to dogs was to rock their legs forward so that their heels would no longer touch the ground. In so doing, they became a "digitigrade" species, meaning that they walk on their digits. This manner of walking, along with longer and stronger forelegs, gives them additional speed. Human beings depend on their ability to manipulate things, so the structure that became the dewclaw in dogs became our thumb. The dog has four digits that make contact with the ground, and the dewclaw is simply a vestigial structure that has been left over by evolution.

Because of these physical changes, the sole of the dog's foot never touches the ground and the dewclaw is too short to be of any functional value. Evolution has an additional trick to further increase the speed of an animal. It involves reconstructing species so that they walk on their tiptoes, which have often developed into hooves. This is what we have in deer and horses. Dogs still do some limited manipulation of things with their paws, so hooves would not be an advantage to them or to those of us who keep our dogs in our homes and would like our wood floors to stay intact.

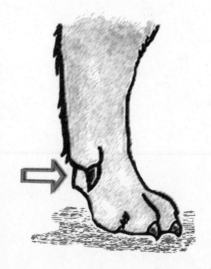

Dewclaws, both front and rear, often cause a bit of worry in dog owners who are afraid the nail will catch on something during a run and be torn off and cause injury. However, some dewclaws are held in tightly against the leg, and with regular nail trimming are unlikely to catch on anything. Others can be loose and floppy, presenting a clear hazard, especially for dogs who like to romp outdoors where roots, trees, and other hazards are common. For that reason, some breeders have the dewclaws removed before the puppy is adopted out, although the majority of dogs are still left with their dewclaws intact.

There is an interesting bit of folklore that keeps some people from removing the dewclaws of their dogs. Many southerners in the United States believe that dogs that are born with dewclaws on their hind feet (which is somewhat rare) have a natural immunity to the venomous effects of snake bites, as long as the dewclaws remain intact. Once, when I was in South Carolina, an old man brought out a favorite hound of his and showed me the dewclaws on her back legs. He explained to me, "She's been snakebit more'an one time, but she's still here 'cause them dewclaws sucked up the poison."

If a Dog Licks My Cut or Wound, Will It Heal Faster?

IN HUMANS AND many other animals, wound licking is an instinctive response to an injury. Dogs, cats, rodents, and primates all lick their own wounds, and dogs will often lick sore places and bleeding patches of skin on their human family members or other people. There is a common folk belief that animal saliva, especially that of dogs, has healing properties for human wounds. Evidence for this belief comes from a number of historical traditions. For example, in ancient Egypt the city of Hardai became known as Cynopolis ("City of Dogs") because in its many temples dedicated to Anubis, the dog-headed guide of the dead, dogs were used as offerings. However, dogs were also used in healing practices there, because the people strongly believed that being licked by a dog, especially in those areas of the body containing sores or lesions, would help to heal the injury or cure the disease causing it. This practice was picked up by the Greeks, and temples dedicated to Asclepius, their god of medicine and healing, often contained dogs trained to lick wounds. In the Middle Ages, Saint Roch was said to have been cured of a plague of sores by being licked by his dog. The value of being licked by a dog is still believed by many cultures to have curative powers. There is even a contemporary

French saying to this effect: *Langue de chien, langue de médecin,* which translates to "A dog's tongue is a doctor's tongue."

The simple mechanical action of a dog's tongue can be helpful in dealing with a wound. The saliva on the tongue loosens any debris that may be on the surface of the wound. Any dirt or other debris will also become attached to the moisture of the saliva; thus, at the very least, the area of the wound will be cleansed.

However, the focus of much scientific research has been on the various antibiotic and helpful compounds that are found in a dog's saliva. The healing powers of saliva have long been suspected, because lesions inside the mouth mend more quickly and scar less than do wounds on the skin. Menno Oudhoff of the University of Amsterdam found simple proteins called "histatins" in saliva. Histatins are well known for their ability to ward off infections.

Some histatins also prompt cells from the skin's surface (called the "epithelium") to close over a wound more quickly. Oudhoff noted, "The first thing that needs to happen for wound healing is to activate the migration of epithelial cells."

Dr. Nigel Benjamin, a clinical pharmacologist with St. Bartholomew's Hospital and the London School of Medicine and Dentistry, claims that licking wounds is as beneficial to humans as it is to animals. His research showed that when saliva comes in contact with skin, nitrite—a natural component of saliva—breaks down into nitric oxide, a chemical compound that is effective in protecting cuts and scratches from bacterial infections. In addition, researchers at the University of Florida at Gainesville have discovered a protein in saliva called "nerve growth factor" (NGF). Wounds doused with NGF healed twice as fast as untreated (that is, unlicked) wounds.

Despite all this evidence, the data on wound licking is not all positive. In the mouths of mammals we also find certain anaerobic bacteria, such as *Pasteurella*. While not harmful in the mouth, *Pasteurella* can cause serious infections when introduced deep into an open wound. There are a number of reports of this happening, and sometimes the results have been extremely negative, causing infections that have resulted in amputations and sometimes death.

One of the interesting aspects of these findings is the suggestion that the helpful chemicals are found not only in the saliva of dogs but also in the saliva of people. Thus, if you're willing to ignore the possible complications in order to gain the healing benefits of having wounds licked, you might not need the assistance of Lassie or Fido. You can actually do it yourself. However, this does not mean that you should indiscriminately offer the benefits of your healing tongue to others. You should be aware of the case of an Oregon teacher who was reprimanded after licking blood from wounds on a track team member's knee, a football player's arm, and a high school student's hand. An Oregon public health officer commented, "We do know that animals lick their own wounds, and it may be that saliva has some healing properties. But my very strong recommendation is that you confine yourself to licking your own wounds."

Why Do Dogs Love Bones?

EVERYONE WHO HAS ever watched a dog chewing on a raw bone has probably noticed how blissful the experience seems to be for him. Even if the bone has very little meat on it and those few clinging meat scraps disappear quickly, the dog will continue to chew on the bone, scraping it or sometimes crushing it when he can get it far enough back into his mouth to work on with his molars. Ultimately, the dog will most likely eat most of the bone, and that is the scientific puzzle. Why would a dog, or any other carnivore, seem to want such an apparently non-nutritious food source to such a degree that it is willing to spend hours working on it, crushing and grinding it so that it can be consumed?

Oddly enough, we get our first inkling as to what's going on here by looking at research on the diet of humans. John D. Speth of the University of Michigan excavated some sites in New Mexico that contained the bones of bison that had been killed around AD 1450. The strange thing about these deposits was that the ancient hunters had left most parts of the female bodies behind, yet they had dragged home as much of the male carcasses as they could carry. So what was wrong with these female bison? A clue comes from the season. While most known prehistoric bison kills happened in fall and winter, these animals were killed in the springtime. What makes female animals unappetizing during the spring turns out to be fat, or rather the lack of it. Pregnant and nursing cows are often severely stressed in the spring because they are carrying a nearly full-grown fetus or nursing a calf, and there is still a long time before there will be enough vegetation to use for adequate foraging. As a result they have to live off of their own fat reserves and their bodies become depleted of fat.

Similar fat depletion can occur when animals are near starvation during cold or dry seasons. At such times an animal's body fat can drop to only a few percent of its total weight (far less than even the leanest cuts of beef). It may surprise many people to learn that a diet made up of almost pure protein actually contains too few calories for adequate nutrition and can even lead to protein poisoning. Apparently these hunters rejected the meat of the female bison because of its low fat content.

To see how inadequate a high-protein diet is in the absence of fat, we can look at a historical incident that occurred in Wyoming during the winter of 1857. A military officer named Randolph Marcy ran out of food and had to march his men all the way to Santa Fe, New Mexico, in order to find adequate provisions. His troops survived by eating their pack animals. Unfortunately, the poor quality of the meat nearly killed the men. Marcy reported, "We tried the meat of horse, colt, and mules, all of which were in a starved condition, and of course not very tender, juicy, and nutritious. We consumed the enormous amount of from five to six pounds of this meat per man daily, but continued to grow weak and thin, until, at the expiration of twelve days, we were able to perform but little labor, and were continually craving for fat meat."

This brings us to the importance of bones in the evolution of carnivores. Seasonal changes swinging between warm and cold in the midlatitudes and wet and dry in the tropics affects the availability of the vegetable matter used as food by the animals that meat eaters depend on as their prey. The last reservoir of fat in an animal undergoing hard times is in the bones. Bone marrow is particularly rich, with more than half of its composition being fat. In addition, bonded to the calcium making up the bone itself is "bone grease," which, although less digestible and concentrated, is still a substantial source of fat. If you are a predator and for some reason your prey is in very poor condition for part of the year, you will greatly increase the value of the meat you have if you can get some fat with it. The fat serves as a sort of nutritional multiplier. Therefore, the ability of carnivores to reach the bone marrow of their prey, and their desire to work at grinding down and consuming the bulk of a bone to access the bone grease, could mean the difference between life and death.

Some carnivores, like the hyena, have specialized teeth for crushing bones. Without these, our domestic dogs have to work harder, but they do have very strong jaws, and even a small dog can work up a bite strength of over two hundred pounds per square inch, which can gradually wear down the largest of bones. Most importantly, evolution has left dogs with the desire to work at getting this source of fat. Evolution uses the trick of making behaviors that are necessary for survival of the individual or species pleasurable (like eating or sex), so it has made the bone-chewing behavior of dogs a great satisfaction for them.

One caution: If you want to give your dog a bone, make sure it's a raw bone. Cooking sweats out the bone grease and often melts away the fat in the bone marrow; furthermore, cooked bones are much more brittle, and eating sharp bone splinters can injure your dog.

Can My Dog Make Me Healthier?

ONE OF THE newest trends in medical research focuses on the relationship between people and their pets, and the effect that this relationship has on the physical well-being of pet owners. Your dog can help tame a stress response that places your health at risk. The medical recognition of the significance of the human-animal bond and its influence on human psychological health is fairly recent.

The research linking heart problems to psychological stress is impressive. For example, a study recently published in the *International Journal of Epidemiology* involved eight years of testing. Research was conducted in the Whitehall district of London on a huge test group (73 percent of all civil servants working in twenty government departments). A variety of stress factors, such as marriage or other family problems, work-related issues, and monetary concerns were considered. The effects of stress were even worse than had been anticipated. Those men who were under psychological stress were 83 percent more likely to have coronary heart disease. Women in the psychologically stressed group had a still-frightening 51 percent increase in heart problems.

Another, larger-scale study conducted in Japan and recently reported in the scientific journal *Circulation* involved more than seventy-three thousand people aged forty to seventy-nine. People who feel stressed on a day-to-day basis have an increased likelihood of dying from stroke or heart disease. Probably the most important finding was that these effects even had an impact on the lowest-risk groups (women who do not have any other risk factors). These stressed-out women were more than twice as likely to die of heart complications than their more mellow peers over the time period studied.

So what does this have to do with your dog? The strong connection between humans and animals has become a subject of serious psychological research. Scientific evidence about the health benefits of such a relationship was first published about thirty years ago when psychologist Alan Beck of Purdue University and psychiatrist Aaron Katcher of the University of Pennsylvania measured what happens physically when a person pets a friendly and famil-

iar dog. They found that the person's blood pressure lowered, heart rate slowed, breathing became more regular, and muscle tension relaxed—all signs of reduced stress.

One study published in the *Journal of Psychosomatic Medicine* not only confirmed these effects, but also showed changes in blood chemistry demonstrating a lower amount of stress-related hormones such as cortisol. These effects seem to be automatic, not requiring any conscious efforts or training on the part of the stressed individual. Perhaps most amazingly, these positive psychological effects are achieved after only five to twenty-four minutes of interacting with a dog—a lot faster than the result from taking most stress-relieving drugs. Compare this to some of the Prozac-type drugs used to deal with stress and depression. These drugs alter the levels of the neurotransmitter serotonin in the body but can take weeks to show any positive effects. Furthermore, the benefits of stress resistance that build up over this long course of medication can be lost with only a few missed doses of the drug. In contrast, petting a dog has a virtually immediate effect and can be done at any time.

A large data base now confirms that pets are good for the health of your heart and may increase the quality of your life and your longevity. The benefits are not just short-term; dogs reduce your stress beyond the period of time that they're present, and they seem to have a cumulative effect. For example, one study of 5,741 people conducted in Melbourne, Australia, found that pet owners had lower levels of blood pressure and cholesterol than did non–pet owners, even when both groups had the same poor lifestyles involving smoking and high-fat diets.

A fascinating study, presented at an American Heart Association Scientific Conference, demonstrated how the addition of a pet to your lifestyle can help. Researchers studied a group of male and female stockbrokers who were already beginning to show the effects of stress and were candidates for medication to lower their blood pressure. The researchers first evaluated the brokers' blood pressure under stressful conditions by giving the research participants timed numerical tasks and asking them to role-play a situation in which they had to talk their way out of an awkward position. In response to these stressful tasks, the participants' average blood pressure shot up to 184/129 millimeters of mercury (any blood pressure of 140/90 or more is considered high).

Each stockbroker was then prescribed the same medication, and half of them also agreed to get a dog or a cat for a pet. Six months later the researchers called them back and administered additional stress tests. Those stockbrokers who had acquired a pet were allowed to keep the pet with them when they took their stress tests and showed a rise in blood pressure that was only half as large as the brokers who had been treated with the medication alone.

Pets can actually help even if you've started to show evidence of heart problems. In an intriguing study published in the *American Journal of Cardiology*, researchers followed more than four hundred patients after they were released from the hospital following a heart attack. One year later the pet owners had a significantly higher survival rate than the non–pet owners.

In the end, it seems that dogs may be a more pleasant and effective way of dealing with stress and coronary problems associated with prolonged stress than either drugs or various therapies. Your pet dog may well be Prozac on paws.

Selected Bibliography and Suggestions for Further Reading

What follows is a listing of some of the sources for material discussed in this book. I tried to include review material whenever possible so that readers can use these citations as a starting point for finding additional research that may interest them. If a reprint or a later edition of a work was consulted, that source rather than the original is listed. The list also includes some of my other books, where more detailed and fully referenced discussions of some of the topics can be found.

B. Adams, A. Chan, H. Callahan, and N. W. Milgram. "The Canine as a Model of Human Cognitive Aging: Recent Developments." *Progress in Neuro-Psychopharmacology & Biological Psychiatry* 24 (2000): 675–92.

E. Adamson, R. G. Beauchamp, M. H. Bonham, S. Coren, M. Fields-Babineau, S. Hodgson, C. Isbell, S. McCullough, G. Spadafori, J. Volhard, W. Volhard, C. Walkowicz, and M. C. Zink. *Dogs All-in-One for Dummies* (Hoboken, NJ: Wiley, 2010).

P. Bateson. "Assessment of Pain in Animals." *Animal Behavior* 42 (1991): 827–39.

G. K. Beauchamp and L. Bartoshuk. *Tasting and Smelling* (San Diego: Academic Press, 1997).

A. M. Beck and A. Y. Katcher. "A New Look at Pet-Facilitated Therapy." *Journal of the American Veterinary Medical Association* 184 (1984): 414–21.

M. Bekoff, C. Allen, and G. M. Burghardt. *The Cognitive Animal: Empirical and Theoretical Perspectives on Animal Cognition* (Cambridge, MA: MIT Press, 2002).

R. E. Brown and D. W. Macdonald. *Social Odours in Mammals* (New York: Clarendon Press, 1985).

W. E. Campbell. *Behavior Problems in Dogs* (Santa Barbara, CA: American Veterinary Publications, 1975).

J. Church and H. Williams. "Another Sniffer Dog for the Clinic?" *Lancet* 358 (2001): 930.

K. M. Cole, and A. Gawlinski. "Animal-Assisted Therapy: The Human-Animal Bond." *AACN Clinical Issues* 11 (2000): 139–49.

J. J. Cooper, C. Ashton, S. Bishop, R. West, D. S. Mills, and R. J. Young. "Clever Hounds: Social Cognition in the Domestic Dog (*Canis familiaris*)." *Applied Animal Behavior Science* 81 (2003): 229–44.

R. Coppinger and L. Coppinger. *Dogs: A Startling New Understanding of Canine Origin, Behavior and Evolution* (New York: Scribner, 2001).

S. Coren. "Barks and Bites: Understanding Aggression—the Signs and Symptoms." *Dog Basics* 6, no. 1 (Spring 2010): 12–14.

S. Coren. "Behind Puppy Dog Eyes: Do You Have a Depressed Dog?" *Puppy and Dog Basics* 5, no. 2 (Fall 2009): 14–16.

S. Coren. "Clairvoyant Canines and Psychic Pooches." *Modern Dog* 3, no. 1 (Spring 2004): 24–28.

S. Coren. "Dogs and Your Health: The China Experiment." *Modern Dog* 8, no. 3 (Fall 2009): 98–100.

S. Coren. "Dogs, Sex and Mathematics." *AnimalSense* 10, no. 1 (Spring/Summer 2009): 22.

S. Coren. "Harmonious Hounds." *Modern Dog* 3, no. 2 (Summer 2004): 18–21.

S. Coren. *How Dogs Think: Understanding the Canine Mind* (New York: Free Press, 2004).

S. Coren. *How to Speak Dog: Mastering the Art of Dog-Human Communication* (New York: Free Press, 2000).

S. Coren. *The Intelligence of Dogs: Canine Consciousness and Capabilities* (New York: Free Press, 2006).

S. Coren. "Laughing Dogs: Does Your Dog Enjoy a Good Joke?" *Modern Dog* 2, no. 4 (Winter 2003): 26–30.

S. Coren. "Mathematical Mutts." *Modern Dog* 3, no. 4 (Winter 2004): 76–79.

S. Coren. *The Modern Dog* (New York: Free Press, 2008).

S. Coren. *The Pawprints of History: Dogs and the Course of Human Events* (New York: Free Press, 2002).

S. Coren. "Pill-Popping Pups: Mood-Altering Drugs and Our Dogs." *Modern Dog* 8, no. 1 (Spring 2009): 90–95.

S. Coren. "Venus, Mars or Pluto?" *Modern Dog* 2, no. 2 (Summer 2003): 30–33.

S. Coren. *Why Does My Dog Act That Way? A Complete Guide to Your Dog's Personality* (New York: Free Press, 2006).

S. Coren. *Why We Love the Dogs We Do* (New York: Free Press, 1998).

S. Coren and S. Hodgson. *Understanding Your Dog for Dummies* (Hoboken, NJ: Wiley, 2007).

V. Csányi. *If Dogs Could Talk* (New York: North Point Press, 2005).

C. Darwin. *The Expression of the Emotions in Man and Animals*, 3rd ed., with an introduction, afterword and commentaries by Paul Ekman (London: Harper Collins, 1998).

N. H. Dodman. *If Only They Could Speak* (New York: Norton, 2002).

J. Donaldson. *Oh Behave!: Dogs from Pavlov to Premack to Pinker* (Wenatchee, WA: Dogwise, 2008).

J. Donaldson. *Train Your Dog Like a Pro* (Hoboken, NJ: Howell, 2010).

D. U. Feddersen-Petersen. "Biology of Aggression in Domestic Dogs." *Deutsche Tieraerztliche Wochenschrift* 108 (2001): 94–101.

J. C. Fentress. "The Covalent Animal: On Bonds and Their Boundaries in Behavioral Research." In *The Inevitable Bond: Examining Scientist-Animal Interactions*, edited by H. Davis and D. Balfour, 44–71. Cambridge University Press, Cambridge, 1992.

E. Friedmann, A. H. Katcher, J. J. Lynch, and S. A. Thomas. "Animal Companions and One-Year Survival of Patients after Discharge from a Coronary Care Unit." *Public Health Reports* 95 (1980): 307–12.

S. D. Gosling, V. S. Y. Kwan, and O. P. John. "A Dog's Got Personality: A Cross-Species Comparative Approach to Personality Judgments in Dogs and Humans." *Journal of Personality and Social Psychology* 85 (2003): 1161–69.

B. Hare, M. Brown, C. Williamson, and M. Tomasello. "The Domestication of Social Cognition in Dogs." *Science* 298 (2002): 1634–36.

B. L. Hart and L. A. Hart. "Selecting Pet Dogs on the Basis of Cluster Analysis of Breed Behavior Profiles and Gender." *Journal of the American Veterinary Medicine Association* 186 (1985): 1181–85.

H. E. Heffner. "Hearing in Large and Small Dogs: Absolute Thresholds and Size of the Tympanic Membrane." *Behavioral Neuroscience* 97 (1983): 310–18.

A. H. Katcher and A. M. Beck. "Dialogue with Animals." *Transactions & Studies of the College of Physicians of Philadelphia* 8 (1986): 105–12.

J. P. Keenan, G. C. Gallup, and D. Falk. *The Face in the Mirror: The Search for the Origins of Consciousness* (New York: HarperCollins, 2003).

R. L. Kitchell. "Taste Perception and Discrimination by the Dog." *Advances in Veterinary Science and Comparative Medicine* 22 (1976): 287–314.

S. R. Lindsay. *Handbook of Applied Dog Behavior and Training.* Vols. 1, *Adaptation and Learning,* and 2, *Etiology and Assessment of Behavior Problems* (Ames: Iowa State University Press, 2000).

P. B. McConnell. "Lessons from Animal Trainers: The Effect of Acoustic Structure on an Animal's Response." In *Perspectives in Ethology,* edited by P. Bateson and P. Kloffer, 165–87, New York: Plenum, 1990.

M. McCulloch, T. Jezierski, M. Broffman, A. Hubbard, K. Turner, and T. Janecki. "Diagnostic Accuracy of Canine Scent Detection in Early- and Late-Stage Lung and Breast Cancers." *Integrative Cancer Therapies* 5 (2006): 30–39.

T. E. McGill. "Amputation of Vibrissae in Show Dogs." *Animal Problems* 1 (1980): 359–61.

L. D. Mech. *The Wolf: The Ecology and Behavior of an Endangered Species* (Minneapolis: University of Minnesota Press, 1981).

P. E. Miller and C. J. Murphy. "Vision in Dogs." *Journal of the American Veterinary Medical Association* 207 (1995): 1623–34.

C. J. Murphy, K. Zadnik, and M. J . Mannis. "Myopia and Refractive Error in Dogs." *Investigative Ophthalmology & Visual Science* 33 (1992): 2459–63.

J. Neitz, T. Geist, and G. S. Jacobs. "Color Vision in the Dog." *Visual Neuroscience* 3 (1989): 119–25.

J. Newby. *The Animal Attraction: Humans and Their Animal Companions* (Sydney, Australia: ABC Books, 1999).

J. S. Odendaal. "Animal-Assisted Therapy—Magic or Medicine?" *Journal of Psychosomatic Research* 49 (2000): 275–80.

K. L. Overall. "Natural Animal Models of Human Psychiatric Conditions: Assessment of Mechanism and Validity." *Progress in Neuro-Psychopharmacology & Biological Psychiatry* 24 (2000): 727–76.

J. Page. *Dogs: A Natural History* (New York: Smithsonian Books, 2007).

P. Pongrácz, A. Miklósi, E. Kubinyi, J. Topául, and V. Csányi. "Interaction between Individual Experience and Social Learning in Dogs." *Animal Behavior* 65 (2003): 595–603.

K. M. Rogers. *First Friend* (New York: St. Martin's Press, 2005).

J. J. Sacks, L. Sinclair, J. Gilchrist, G. C. Golab, and R. Lockwood. "Breeds of Dogs Involved in Fatal Human Attacks in the United States between 1979 and 1998." *Journal of the American Veterinary Medical Association* 217 (2000): 836–40.

J. P. Scott and J. L. Fuller. *Genetics and the Social Behavior of the Dog* (Chicago: University of Chicago Press, 1965).

C. Short and A. V. Poznak. *Animal Pain* (New York: Strawson, 1992).

K. Svartberg and B. Forkman. "Personality Traits in the Domestic Dog (*Canis familiaris*)." *Applied Animal Behavior Science* 79 (2002): 133–55.

L. Watson. *Jacobson's Organ and the Remarkable Nature of Smell* (New York: Norton, 2000).

R. West and R. J. Young. "Do Domestic Dogs Show Any Evidence of Being Able to Count?" *Animal Cognition* 5 (2002): 183–86.

C. M. Willis, S. M. Church, C. M. Guest, W. A. Cook, N. McCarthy, A. J. Bransbury, M. R. Church, and J. C. Church. "Olfactory Detection of Human Bladder Cancer by Dogs: Proof of Principle Study." *British Medical Journal* 329 (2004): 712.

R. Wiseman, M. Smith, and J. Milton. "Can Animals Detect When Their Owners Are Returning Home? An Experimental Test of the 'Psychic Pet' Phenomenon." *British Journal of Psychology* 89 (1998): 453–62.

T. D. Wyatt. *Pheromones and Animal Behaviour: Communication by Smell and Taste* (New York: Cambridge University Press, 2003).

Index